5/21

THE AOC
GENERATION

THE AOC GENERATION

HOW MILLENNIALS ARE SEIZING
POWER AND REWRITING THE RULES
OF AMERICAN POLITICS

DAVID FREEDLANDER

BEACON PRESS
BOSTON

BEACON PRESS
Boston, Massachusetts
www.beacon.org

Beacon Press books
are published under the auspices of
the Unitarian Universalist Association of Congregations.

24 23 22 21   8 7 6 5 4 3 2 1

This book is printed on acid-free paper that meets the uncoated paper
ANSI/NISO specifications for permanence as revised in 1992.

Text design and composition by Kim Arney

Library of Congress Cataloging-in-Publication Data

Names: Freedlander, David, author.
Title: The AOC generation : how millennials are seizing power and rewriting
    the rules of American politics / David Freedlander.
Description: Boston : Beacon Press, [2021] | Includes bibliographical references.
Identifiers: LCCN 2020030890 (print) | LCCN 2020030891 (ebook) |
    ISBN 9780807036433 (hardcover) | ISBN 9780807036440 (ebook)
Subjects: LCSH: Ocasio-Cortez, Alexandria, 1989– | Generation Y—Political
    activity—United States. | United States—Politics and government.
Classification: LCC E901.1.O27 F74 2021 (print) | LCC E901.1.O27 (ebook) |
    DDC 305.20973/0905—dc23
LC record available at https://lccn.loc.gov/2020030890
LC ebook record available at https://lccn.loc.gov/2020030891

For my girls:
Lily, Claribel, and Rosa

CONTENTS

INTRODUCTION   The Happy Hour   •   1

CHAPTER 1   Sandy   •   19

CHAPTER 2   The District   •   49

CHAPTER 3   Her Revolution   •   79

CHAPTER 4   The Left of the Possible   •   105

CHAPTER 5   The Civil War to Come   •   125

CHAPTER 6   The Storytellers   •   149

CHAPTER 7   The Green New World   •   173

Epilogue   •   203
Acknowledgments   •   211
Notes   •   215

THE HAPPY HOUR

Summer was nearly over, there was a slight chill in the air portending the coming of fall, and New York City had begun to empty out for the Labor Day 2017 weekend. But one bar, just below ground level on a side street in the city's East Village, was packed, as it was most Thursday evenings. That's where a couple of dozen leftist political organizers and advocates started routinely gathering at a happy hour hosted by Sean McElwee.

McElwee, then just twenty-four, looked like a twelve-year-old inflated to adult-size, dressed in a too-small T-shirt with a baseball cap askew atop his head. But his weekly happy hours at the dingy dive—he asked that the name of the bar not be used because right-wing protesters might crash it—quickly became an essential stop for the city's activist class in the months after Donald Trump's surprise win in November 2016. Gathered most Thursday nights at the bar were newly minted socialists, tired campaign workers, government staffers, think-tank types, and others devoted to a wide variety of progressive and leftist causes. To be there and to be over thirty would be considered ancient.

McElwee could often be found at a table in the back, where a steady stream of friends, well-wishers, and journalists stopped by. When I met him that evening, he berated me for not using his quotes in a story I had written. He also predicted that one day his own children would find him to be a moral degenerate for eating meat and said that he was working on building a world where eco-terrorists could receive veterans benefits.

On the night at August's end, one of the people who swung by was a little-known long-shot congressional candidate named Alexandria Ocasio-Cortez, looking impossibly put together in a black dress with a white quilted blazer and more than a little out-of-place in a neon-lit bar that hadn't changed its decor in forty-five years.

She was there at the invitation of McElwee, who had been hyping online the slew of left-leaning challengers running for offices up and down the slate, and inviting most of them to come drink with him and his pals, part of a renewed interest in electoral politics by a mostly younger generation horrified at the prospect of a Trump presidency. He direct-messaged her on Twitter at a time when Ocasio-Cortez had only a few hundred followers and invited her to come by.

At the bar, she put Led Zeppelin on the jukebox and lamented how New York's notoriously closed electoral system was making it nearly impossible for a candidate like her, a young Latina from the Bronx, to compete, especially against the behemoth she was running against, Joe Crowley. He was not just the likely next Speaker of the House of Representatives but also the head of the Queens County Democratic Party, which meant there was a whole apparatus of election lawyers and judges in his thrall and that the entire city's political class was in his corner.

People who were there that night remember Ocasio-Cortez as being, for a politician, unusually interested in hearing about what the different activists had done in their various lines of work.

"What I remember is that she just kind of lit up the room," said Matthew Miles Goodrich, an environmental organizer who had just begun to work with the Sunrise Movement, a youth-led organization founded in 2017 and dedicated to slowing climate change and making issues of environmental justice central to the US political debate after decades of neglect. "I went to Sean's happy hour every week, and there were a lot of candidates coming through, and it was just immediately clear that this person was pretty fantastic."[1]

While most candidates who came through seemed to do a quick appraisal of who would be helpful to them and who wouldn't be, Ocasio-Cortez seemed genuinely excited to be surrounded by organizers working to build political and social movements, according to those who were there, and she pelted people with questions about the details of their work.

By that summer night, it was already clear that something was afoot in America. This book is the story of that something. It is the story, in part, of Alexandria Ocasio-Cortez, of how she rose from the life of an adrift twenty-something making her way in New York to an overnight sensation, the likes of which the political world had never seen, becoming an icon of pop culture in the process. But no person, no matter how dynamic, is the product only of their own will and talent. All of us are pushed quietly along by thousands of unseen hands, are the product of society and circumstance, the place we were born into and the people we come to know. And so this isn't just the story of Ocasio-Cortez, it is the story of the people who powered her rise, and the circumstances in the city and in the nation that made her rise possible.

Ocasio-Cortez was the youngest woman ever elected to Congress, and her appearance on Capitol Hill was seen correctly as a harbinger of a new, ascendant generation, one pulling the nation leftward, fed up with politics as usual, and fearful of a future in which ecological catastrophe, widening inequality, and the rise of illiberal populism threatened life as they had come to know it. They were the best educated and most diverse generation in the nation's history, and in the wake of the election of Donald Trump many of them decided that if anything was going to change, they would have to do it themselves. Ocasio-Cortez was one of those young people who faced that choice, and she was the beneficiary of similar choices thousands of young people made who decided that if anything was ever going to change, they would have to change it themselves. This story is the story of both them, and of her.

It is not an endorsement of their tactics or their ideology. I am a political reporter, and so it is rather an examination of a new force that looks set to have a large role in our politics for decades to come, and a look at how Ocasio-Cortez stepped into a moment that was waiting for her to seize it. I live in Ocasio-Cortez's district, and watched as her long-shot campaign pulled off one of the upsets of the century, and I interviewed her when she was campaigning and desperate for any kind of coverage. Neither Ocasio-Cortez nor her office participated in this book. I interviewed her twice while she was in Congress for a story for *New York Magazine* and her comments to me in this book come from that conversation. I interviewed dozens of people who knew her at various times in her life and who were willing to share their memories of her, and dozens and dozens more who got engaged in politics around 2016 and helped make this moment, the Ocasio-Cortez moment, possible.

The biggest single force that helped make AOC possible was Bernie Sanders. Without Sanders, there would almost certainly be no Alexandria Ocasio-Cortez. An avowed democratic socialist, he ran one of the most vocally left-wing campaigns in US political history. More surprising, it nearly worked. Sanders, a senator from Vermont, almost won the Democratic primary, despite running against an opponent, Hillary Clinton, with vastly more resources and almost the entire Democratic Party supporting her. Sanders won more than two million votes from eighteen- to twenty-nine-year-olds in the 2016 primary, more than either Hillary Clinton or Donald Trump *combined.*[2] In Iowa, the first state to vote in the Democratic primary, Sanders beat Clinton among this cohort by seventy points (84 percent to 14 percent), according to a caucus entrance poll.[3]

In New York, despite being the home state of Hillary Clinton, voters eighteen to twenty-nine turned out in record numbers toward the end of the primary, and Sanders beat Clinton among them by thirty points. Tens of thousands of people poured into his rallies, and tens of thousands more signed up to volunteer.

Sanders was by no means the first left-wing candidate to run for president. Every campaign saw at least one candidate pledging to "represent the Democratic wing of the Democratic Party" or restore the party's liberal soul: Dennis Kucinich in 2004 and 2008, Howard Dean in 2004, Ralph Nader in 2000, and Jerry Brown in 1992. They each promised to get money out of politics, to end foreign entanglements, to reform America's messed up healthcare system, and to close the widening gap between rich and poor. But although they each generated excitement, particularly from a curious political press corps, they each faded fairly quickly into irrelevance.

And none had views that were as left wing as Sanders, who called for a political revolution that would include free college, nationalized healthcare, massive new taxes on the rich, and an end to the nation's reliance on fossil fuels.

Sanders was in some ways an odd figure to ignite the young. White-haired, balding, and rumpled, he turned seventy-five years old in 2016 and had none of the coolness or charisma that Barack Obama, another candidate who thrilled the young, possessed when he ran eight years earlier.

Speaking broadly of generations is difficult. They are too vast and amorphous, too varied in their demographic data points, and they send conflicting signals about their desires and needs, making it difficult to talk about them in any serious and scientific way.

Still, some things can be discerned. Young people who were just starting middle school on the day that terrorists flew commercial aircrafts into the Twin Towers graduated from college into a labor market with the worst unemployment rate since the Great Depression. They, in some respects, grew up in an era as safe and as comfortable as any in US history, a time of rising standards of living, decreases in crime, increases in life expectancy, rising educational standards, and limited social upheavals. Technology that would have been inconceivable a generation ago meant conveniences and options for education—but also distractions—that even a few years prior would have seemed like something out of science fiction. This generation saw the election of the first African American president, the legalization of gay marriage, women entering the workforce and the ranks of higher education at rates unseen before in US history, while the country grew more diverse and more accepting of diversity.

But they also saw not just the terror attacks in 2001 but two wars and a devastating recession, widening inequality, the rise of the surveillance state, college becoming increasingly unaffordable, a grisly procession of school and workplace shootings, and a steady succession of deadly wildfires, hurricanes, and floods that revealed the depth of the climate catastrophe.

In the first decades of the twenty-first century, the Republican Party veered sharply to the right, embracing positions that were well outside the mainstream on issues like gun control, abortion, gay rights, and the environment. The GOP grew further enthralled by trickle-down economics, cutting taxes for the wealthy and for corporations, and attempting to shred the social safety net. The party deepened its alliance with evangelical Christians, embarking on a campaign of public-facing religiosity, breaking down the walls between church and state, and promoting restrictions on personal freedoms around sex and marriage, which were increasingly out of step with a rising generation that had been taught that tolerance and respect for difference were bedrock American values. The Republican Party not only embarked on two ruinous wars abroad but instituted a system of extrajudicial killings, torture, surveillance, and secret prisons around the world, which some on the right spoke of in terms of a religious crusade. Over time the party discarded many of these values as Trump seized control of it, and the spirit of the party became animated by white nationalism and an anti-immigrant fervor, breaking down a global order that had left America as the world's sole superpower since the fall of the Soviet Union (along with the rights and responsibilities that came along with it). Along the way, the party developed an ethos that favored sticking a finger in the eye of liberal pieties and tweaking what they presumed to be an overbearing culture of political correctness over specific policy positions or even moral values.

Democrats and liberals spent most of the early years of the twenty-first century on the defensive. Many felt they were living in an era that was shaped more by Ronald Reagan or even Barry Goldwater than by Bill Clinton or Barack Obama, a time when, as Clinton proclaimed, "The era of big government is over." After he was elected, Obama failed to meaningfully clamp down on Wall Street's excesses in the wake of the 2008 crash, proposed cutting Social Security and Medicare, acquiesced to GOP-purported concerns over taxes and deficits, continued much of Bush's war on terror, and drew such a hard line on immigration that critics labeled him the "deporter in chief."

After the crash of 2008, the primary vehicle for protest came from the Right, even though the crisis was presided over by a Republican president and precipitated by Wall Street. The Tea Party swept the Republicans into power and moved the party even further to the right as millions of people, fed up with politics as usual, pushed for new leaders outside of the familiar political circles.

The generation of people in their twenties during this period veered sharply to the left. A *USA Today* poll of Americans under the age of thirty-five in January 2016 found that, by a seventy-point margin, respondents thought the United States should transition to mostly clean or renewable energy by 2030, and by a more than two-to-one margin called for greater investments in public transportation. Eighty-two percent of young people surveyed called for all gun buyers to undergo background checks, three-quarters called for police to wear body cameras, and two-thirds called for reduced prison sentences for nonviolent offenders.[4]

A 2018 YouGov survey found that by a nine-point margin eighteen- to twenty-nine-year-olds had a favorable view of socialism (in comparison, Americans sixty-four and older had an unfavorable view by a thirty-one-point margin), while a third of young people said they would be comfortable voting for a socialist candidate.[5]

A YouGov poll the next year had even more striking numbers: It showed that 50 percent of millennials (and 49 percent of Generation Z) had a very or somewhat favorable opinion of capitalism and that 70 percent of millennials were likely or extremely likely to vote for a socialist candidate, numbers that were twice as high as any other generation (except, again, for members of Gen Z, of whom 64 percent said they would be likely to vote for a socialist). Meanwhile, only a slight majority—57 percent—of millennials said that the Declaration of Independence provided a better guarantee of freedom and equality than *The Communist Manifesto*.[6]

There were some category errors involved here or, at least, some category confusion. A 2018 survey by the Public Religion Research Institute asked respondents to define socialism as either a "system of government that provides citizens with health insurance, retirement support, and access to a free higher education" or as "a system where the government controls key parts of the economy, such as utilities, transportation and communications industries."[7] Young Americans chose the first definition, one that corresponded with how Sanders described his ideology and one that described the economic and political system of many countries across northern Europe.[8]

Some sociologists, economists, and pollsters suggested that the reason for this sharp break to the left was not that young people were struggling but that they were comfortable. The concept of "the revolution of rising expectations" became part of the social science literature in the years after World War II. The phrase was used to suggest that people rise up not when they have hit the lowest rung of society, but when their lot has begun to improve. The problem, however, is that they don't rise fast enough.

As McElwee tells it, as we hunched over a couple of beers in the back corner of the bar, this is nonsense. The reason that his happy hours became so popular, and the reason that so many young people turned sharply to the left and became active in social causes and politics, is because of an increase in educational attainment among his generation twinned with the effects of the recession.

A common explanation for how the financial crisis of 2008 impacted young people is that as they came into an empty job market with mountains of student debt, then moved left as they took jobs beneath their education level that mired them further in debt. But that was only part of it, McElwee says. More importantly, the recession changed economic views among elite opinion makers; no longer could one credibly argue on op-ed pages that the economy was functioning for most Americans. The recession allowed new ideas to enter mainstream America.

"People don't realize that a lot of politics is about elite persuasion," he said. "The recession disrupted the center-right ideology that had been dominant for forty years. *That's* the world we inherited."

At the beginning of the Trump era, McElwee had become one of the leading voices of this new generation of young political activists, someone who harnessed the power of social media to get issues previously thought to be outside the bounds of acceptable political debate onto the agenda of major political figures. He began to call himself "An Overton Window Mover," a reference to an idea conceived by Joseph P. Overton, the head of the conservative Mackinac Center for Public Policy in the 1990s. Overton showed potential donors the think tank's brochure, explaining that there is a range of ideas—from the broadly acceptable to the fringe or the unacceptable. His job, he explained, was to move items from the latter category into the former, giving politicians a broader range of policy ideas to consider. It didn't mean the ideas would become law, but it did mean they would now be debated alongside other solutions and would consequently shift what was previously considered outlandish into the mainstream.

McElwee did this almost single-handedly with his call to abolish Immigration and Customs Enforcement, cornering politicians over social media to take a stand on the issue and encouraging his nearly one hundred thousand followers to do the same at a time when few were talking about it. It didn't work—ICE still exists—but it did mean that Americans began to look more critically at its vast immigration enforcement agencies, and allowed previously left-wing positions on immigration to seem relatively moderate by comparison. When Ocasio-Cortez won her upset victory over Crowley, McElwee was at the Bronx pool hall where her victory party was held and got her to promise him to introduce legislation that would abolish ICE and to set up a congressional investigation into the agency's abuses on her first day in office.

He was in many ways an unlikely figure in a movement that was both very diverse and largely composed of people with degrees from elite institutions of higher education. McElwee grew up in the town of Ledyard, Connecticut, near New London. His first political engagement was witnessing fights over keeping the local naval base open. He moved to New York to attend King's College, a school founded by the Campus Crusade for Christ in the 1950s, and where student houses are named after figures like Ronald Reagan, Margaret Thatcher, and Queen Elizabeth I. He chose King's only because he saw an advertisement for it in the one magazine his family subscribed to, *World*, an evangelical publication.

McElwee was, at the time, what he calls "a rebellion Libertarian," one who interned at the Reason Foundation and at Fox Business Network, but he would go home to his rural, working-class area of Connecticut, where he saw friends whose mothers were addicted to methadone and where he came to realize that libertarianism didn't address the scope of society's problems, nor did it allow for how the circumstances of someone's birth could affect their life path.

McElwee got a job at Demos, a left-wing think tank in New York, and had the idea of having the city's lefties get together every Thursday because having productive conversations about politics over Twitter was becoming impossible and because "I fucking hate books."

"Books are stupid. Think about books from the perspective of an economist," he said, describing a book written by a hedge fund billionaire that advised people on how to get rich. "I'd be a chump if I thought I could learn how to make a billion dollars like he did from a book. If I could, then how would he be able to make a billion dollars? The world is zero-sum. I don't like knowledge that you can find in a book. I like knowledge that you can't find in a book. After college you shouldn't read a book, you should try to gain power. The things that are valuable are the things that people are trying to keep secret, by definition."

As a left-wing activist, however, he was invited to a seemingly never-ending number of book launch parties. "But I don't read books, so I didn't want to go to a book launch party, so I thought to start a happy hour. That way people can get drunk without the excuse. I like creating networks, creating community. The motherfuckers in DC are having happy hours all the time. Why shouldn't the Left?" Get people together, in other words, toss in a few drinks, and they will tell you what they really know and maybe even what they don't want other people to learn.

After the election of Trump, it became clear that whatever strategy the Left was pursuing wasn't working. Too many of his compatriots seemed to think that the point of politics was to write tweets and take stances that made them feel better about themselves, not to actually pass laws or attain power. And so McElwee started his own think tank and policy shop called Data for Progress, designed to show which left-wing ideas were actually more popular than people realized and which weren't, and to provide some intellectual ballast to an emerging political movement on the left.

As we sat in the bar, McElwee explained his thinking. "Why do we keep losing elections?" he said. "That's my question. We lose elections because a lot of our ideas are not popular. I may love Medicare for All, but the question is not what do I love; it is what will get us to 51 percent. You run on your strongest message. Not even what you want to do but the thing that will get you across the finish line. And I came to realize that one of the problems the Left has is that we don't just want to see our candidates win. We want to see our candidates win by running on our issues and we want them to run by talking about our issues in the way we want them to talk about them. And you can't have all of that. At some point you have to figure out a way to talk about issues in a way voters care about. And that is the ultimate narcissism that is preventing us from gaining larger political power."

A 2020 study by Data for Progress found that "today's young voters are strikingly liberal and Democratic, to a degree that is not comparable to any past generation," and while there is some evidence that age cohorts get gradually more conservative over time, that evidence is often overstated and can depend on economic circumstances. The study pointed out that much of what tends to make voters more conservative—homeownership, easing into a higher income bracket, or getting married—are precisely things that are happening much later for this cohort, largely because of how our economy has come to function. Polling that has tracked millennials over the last several election cycles finds them not only to be largely Democratic and left-leaning but growing more Democratic and further left-leaning over the past fifteen years.[9]

These findings suggest that "millennials will probably end up somewhat more conservative in the future than they are now, but their politically formative years have largely already passed."

For millennials, this formative period was defined by the failures of two Republican Presidents (W. Bush and Trump) and the success of a popular Democrat (Obama). Research has shown that millennials' views on racial justice have been positively shaped by the Black Lives Matter movement. Other research suggests that recessions during an individual's formative political years durably increases support for more redistribution. Millennials have already experienced two incredibly destructive recessions, punctuating an economy characterized by increasing income volatility, increasing underemployment, and meager wage growth which has never managed to reach its high in the late 90's before any millennial had entered the labor market as an adult. As far as formative experiences go, these are pretty well optimized to produce a left-leaning cohort.[10]

Millennials, Data for Progress points out, have come of age in a world in which government policies inflate housing worth, locking them out of home buying. Stagnant wages, high housing costs, high returns on stocks, free-flowing credit, and mass incarceration were used in place of the kind of social safety net most rich countries enjoyed.

The policies that created a bloc of older voters who use the political system to fiercely defend the value of the assets they hold also created a bloc of asset-less younger voters who have no stake in an economic system that suppresses their wages and piles them with educational and consumer debt in order to fuel growth in asset prices. In fact, the current moment in politics gives us a window into an alternate version of history. Without rising home and stock prices, it is easy to imagine that middle class voters would never have tolerated the tepid economic growth and abysmal wage growth that have typified the neoliberal period.

Politics is now dominated by a new social class of petty capitalists, which includes a large number of older blue collar workers who depend on seeing returns on their property for financial security. At the opposite end of the political spectrum, a new class of grand proletarians is emerging; well educated young professionals who do not own property and whose fears of downward mobility are driving their demands for the US to adopt some semblance of social democracy. Combined with the fact that millennials are the most diverse and best educated generation at a time where racial justice movements are gaining momentum and partisanship is sorting along the lines of racism and xenophobia; we have a perfect storm for producing the stark and completely unprecedented age polarization that exists in politics today.[11]

The weeks and months after Trump's election saw an explosion of energy from the Left. People who had never attended a protest took to the streets. Americans who were never much interested in politics swarmed teach-ins at churches, community centers, and living rooms to figure out what they could do to curb the power of someone who voiced disdain for so many seemingly incontrovertible

American values like a free press, a pluralistic democracy, a respect for dissent, and for opposing parties.

Those months were a heady time for the American Left, which had spent decades on the margins of US politics. There had been important victories for civil rights, gay rights, and women as the culture at large grew more welcoming and accepting. Equal rights for all gradually became a cornerstone of American civic life, but at the same time inequality widened, the labor movement shriveled even further, and college and healthcare costs spiraled upward.

Despite protests against climate change and widespread awareness of the topic, the nation remained overly reliant on fossil fuels, global temperatures rose, and the polar ice caps continued to melt. Even as the effects of climate change became a lived reality in many parts of the country—with devastating fires ravaging the West, floods submerging parts of the South, and record-setting droughts and heat waves killing scores—the federal government failed to address the issue except in the most cursory of ways. Gun violence continued to plague much of the nation, and even as school shootings occurred with grim regularity, including a classroom of first graders murdered a few days before Christmas in 2012, no laws were changed at the federal level.

Throughout most of the first decades of the twenty-first century, liberals and leftists appeared to have acquired cultural hegemony, spreading their values through the popular culture of TV, movies, and music but holding very little by way of political power. Some of this was due to the fact that efforts to get money out of politics and reform the culture of lobbyist- and corporate-interest-driven government—itself another generational cause of the Left in the years after Watergate—had been set back considerably over the previous decade and a half. Money had become such a large part of US politics that it threatened to drown out other forms of political engagement. Presidential campaigns had become billion-dollar enterprises. Part of the job of being in any elective office was spending a large portion of the day dialing potential donors for contributions. After the Supreme Court's 2010 decision in the *Citizens United* case, what little remained of campaign finance regulation was gutted, allowing corporations to spend with impunity. Thus was born a new class of uber donors to political campaigns and the proliferation of lightly regulated super PACs, which displaced much of the work of political parties and campaigns, as politics became awash in difficult-to-trace "dark money."

In the 1950s and 1960s, public protest helped bring about massive social change, including ending segregation, halting the Vietnam War, and heralding ever increasing rights for women and LGBT people. But in a reactionary era, those tactics had begun to grow stale. There were marches for nuclear disarmament and ending apartheid in South Africa, hunger strikes for increasing diversity on college campuses, and die-ins for increased funding for education and medical research. But even as tens of thousands of Americans took to the streets to protest the Iraq War or to support measures to curb climate change or even to occupy public parks to protest against a government that seemed to care more about the health of financial markets than of its citizens, the political needle scarcely moved at all. No meaningful liberal legislation was passed. For many left activists, their primary political participation involved showing up to rallies or campaign events to shout down speakers, something that the politicians welcomed, since it made them seem sympathetic and got crowds on their sides, while allowing their opponents to come across as boors who prefer booing to honest debate. The abandonment of the political sphere by many on the Left meant that the political sphere could abandon the Left in turn.

The Sanders campaign of 2016, with its electric energy, massive crowds, millions in small-dollar fundraising contributions, and millions of votes, despite—or because of—being the most avowedly left-wing political campaign in thirty years, began to change the calculus. Leftists realized that if they wanted power, and if they wanted to enact the policies they purported to believe, they would need to engage in political fights, and more importantly, they would need to start winning them.

This is the realization that political activists on the Left came to post-Bernie and especially post-Trump. If politics before 2016 had been seen as grubby or impure, a matter of cutting deals and abandoning goals to build a coalition, it gradually became clear that in 2016 that kind of deal making would be the ground upon which battles would be won or lost.

"I came to realize at some point that the point of all of this was to pass laws," McElwee said. "We didn't have a lot of power, and we didn't have theories of power or ways to leverage the power we did have. We should have more power than the rest of the Democratic coalition. We are highly educated. We live in metropolitan areas where elites gather. We have more money than the average Democrat and more access to people in power. We should be running the place, but instead we have way more podcasters than other parts of the Democratic coalition, have way more people posting on social media, have way more people getting their politics out by writing bad takes. But wouldn't we be better off if we had a half dozen House members and a handful of senators who were sympathetic to our views?"

McElwee distinguished between "activists," gesturing to indicate air quotes as we sat in the bar, and actual activists. In his young career, he had worked with both. The second group doesn't spend as much time yelling on Twitter or even participating in rallies, but they work with people in affected communities, people who do either direct service work or who advocate on behalf of their constituencies.

"They don't just throw anything out there. They are strategic. They made deals with politicians and they don't get behind challengers who won't make deals," McElwee said. "If your job is to yell at politicians, then your job is easy. If you want to make your job hard, you sometimes don't yell at politicians, and you figure out how you can gain power in the system."

This was the system that Ocasio-Cortez, a few months ago in the very bar where we were sitting, decided she wanted to be a part of. She, too, had turned away from politics in her early twenties. As the effects of the Great Recession settled in, she worked waitressing and bartending, putting aside other dreams she had for her life. She was someone who took the bus home from college to vote for Obama in her first election but had gradually soured on him, becoming caught up in a series of grassroots movements that swept the nation in the wake of Obama's reelection in 2012: the fight for Dreamers to achieve full legal status, the fight for fair wages for working people, and the Movement for Black Lives.

She was outrageously young when she decided to run for Congress and, more to the point, outrageously uncredentialed, having never served in elective office, with no real experience in government, and very little experience working on behalf of the community where she lived in Queens and the Bronx.

But Ocasio-Cortez was part of a generation that lionized the outsider and the amateur—the engineer who built a mainframe on his computer or the novelist who wrote a best seller after the kids went to sleep. She grew up to believe, as many in her generation did, that the world was theirs for the taking, that the people in charge didn't know as much as they let on. Her cohort valued people just like her, those who had been previously marginalized—women, people of color, those who rose above the circumstances of their life.

And when Ocasio-Cortez won, she became the avatar of this new generation, and for good reason. She was an avowed democratic socialist, a woman of color, and the youngest woman ever elected to Congress. She was an electric speaker and displayed a fluency on social media that was rare for a politician. She wasn't all that American politics was, but she was surely all that American politics was becoming.

"Those of us in our twenties or younger, just coming into the electorate now, I don't think people are ready for us," McElwee said. "It is the most liberal generation ever polled. We could grow much more conservative over time and we would still be the most liberal generation ever polled. We are going to be deeply fucking with American politics for a very long time to come."

CHAPTER 1

SANDY

It was Martin Luther King Jr. Day, 2011, and Sandy, as she was then known, was a college senior, and the lone student on the Boston University campus invited to speak at the university's annual remembrance ceremony. King got his doctorate at Boston University, and so King Day was a more solemn celebration at BU than it was at most other elite Northeastern schools.

Ocasio-Cortez was nowhere near the polished speaker she would become while in Congress. Still baby-faced and in glasses, she adopted the tone and cadence of a preacher and set out to address the question that was the theme of the program for the day: "Can This Generation Be Great?"

Her answer, though, was not *whether* but *how*.

"This generation does not consist of people currently between the ages of eighteen and thirty-five. No, it certainly does not," she said.[1] "This generation consists of all people who choose to be young at this time. It is a much smaller group. As they say, it is far less work to curse the rain than it is to sow a seed. Giving up is easy. It is living out our imaginations that takes work but to live in that world is to be young and, like greatness, the roots of youth is not a circumstance but a choice. There are no chosen ones.

"There are only those who choose. It is never too late. We can choose to be great. We can choose to be young, for greatness is reserved for the delinquents."

Hers was a generation that had been brought up to believe they could bend the world to their will. If something did not match their expectations, the solution was to change the thing, not their expectations. They had been brought up to believe they were unique and that the purpose of life was giving that uniqueness to the world. "At the moment we discover the brilliance of our individual faculties, at the instant we feel the slightest unease that life, as it is supposed to be, is not life as we intended, we are obligated to leap into the shelters of our creative genius," she told the audience. "To do otherwise, to yield to the forces of circumstance guarantees a death far worse than that of a beatless heart—that of a subordinate spirit."

Ocasio-Cortez laid out ideas in that speech that would come to animate her political life six years later. She spoke of a world where, "in the Bronx, children . . . cannot count by coincidence of their zip code" and where "Virginian couples turned from courthouses by chances of their gender, where the ideas of Plato and Jefferson become as attainable as the items behind a Park Avenue window."

She surely never intended her speech, an honor bestowed upon a campus leader, to be heard as something delivered from the voice of her generation. But in light of what the coming years were to bring, it can easily be read that way.

"There are so many possibilities to take a stake in at this very moment," she said on that afternoon in Boston. "It is not only us who are young. The world is young as well. Banana farmers in the rural Congo can testify to that in a text message. A five-year-old in Boston can easily connect with another in Calcutta. Five hundred million people are all connected to one virtual social network. This is what the dawn of an era looks like."

Ocasio-Cortez studied economics and international relations at Boston University, a sprawling campus bisected by Commonwealth Avenue and across the Charles River from MIT. Boston University, with its thirty-four thousand-strong enrollment, looks and sounds like a public university and, until the mid-twentieth century, was largely a commuter college for Bostonians. But in the years since, it has grown into a mid-tier university largely attended by Northeasterners with enough money to afford its annual $55,000 price tag.

Ocasio-Cortez studied economics and international relations. But she really found her home at a BU multicultural arts and social justice community space called the Howard Thurman Center for Common Ground.

Thurman was a Florida-born pastor, the grandson of slaves, and a philosopher, theologian, and spiritual mentor to a later generation of civil rights leaders, including Martin Luther King Jr. He was a dean at Boston University, served on the faculty of the university's school of theology, and authored nearly two dozen books.

The core of Thurman's teaching centered around the notion that African Americans and other oppressed people needed to find a spiritual, internal (and eternal) strength to survive their oppressors. In doing so, they could overcome, and help others overcome, their surroundings. His insight was the same for white Americans who were part of the power structure—that by tapping into something deeper within themselves, they could let go of some of their insistence on their own superiority.

Thurman's sayings plastered the walls of the student center: "Don't ask yourself what the world needs. Ask yourself what makes you come alive, and go do that, because what the world needs is people who have come alive," and "Keep the dream alive, for as long as a man has a dream in his heart he cannot lose the significance of living."

It was a place that attracted a certain type of student, one who largely didn't come to BU from a northeastern prep school or from a wealthy, all-white suburb. The students who gathered there, like Sandy, had parents who moved to the mainland from Puerto Rico, or were born in Africa and adopted by Americans, or were the children of immigrants from Latin America or Asia, or were working-class Midwesterners going through personal hardship. Sandy had close friends from all those groups.

The students would gather every Friday for "Coffee and Conversation," hosted by one of the faculty leaders and catered by a local coffee shop. Conversations would touch on the kind of campus third rails that most people know to avoid: race, class, politics, sex, and the various controversies on campus. Ocasio-Cortez met her longtime partner, Riley Roberts, at BU. He was a regular at the Coffee and Conversations, too, and several participants remembered the two as quite the pair, with Roberts often playing the role of devil's advocate in the group, the politically incorrect provocateur with the libertarian bent, in order to break the consensus of the group.

"The Howard Thurman Center is a place to come when you don't exactly know where to go," said Raul Fernandez, now an associate dean and a member of the select board of Brookline, an upscale Boston suburb, in a video on the center's website explaining what it is. "I think of it as the Times Square of BU."

"If you want to meet cool people that want to be somebody in the future and want to be doing something, it is at the Howard Thurman Center," added another student.

Ocasio-Cortez is in the video too. She is sitting on a couch, reading *All Souls: A Family Story from Southie*, a 1999 memoir by Michael Patrick MacDonald about growing up in the high-poverty, high-crime Irish Catholic neighborhoods of South Boston. "This is a place to learn about life in different ways that you don't learn in other places," she said.

I spoke with dozens of people who knew Ocasio-Cortez in college or in the years before—as she grew up in Yorkville, New York, a prosperous suburb north of New York City—or as she tried to make her way in the world as a young college graduate in a city still shrugging off the effects of the Great Recession. Some knew her well, and some just observed her from afar, but they told pretty much the same thing: the young Ocasio-Cortez was not different from the person who seemed to emerge fully formed on the national stage in the summer of 2018. They describe a girl and a young woman who was exceptionally smart, quick on her feet, articulate, determined to make a difference in the world, and genuinely decent and caring, concerned for the inequities in the world and for other people. I spoke with a number of people who described themselves as her friend but who weren't among her closest friends, and yet they described a relationship that is usually reserved only for close friends: visiting Sandy for the weekend at college, staying with her family for Thanksgiving, meeting up for dinner when passing through New York in the years after college, going to Yorktown for a pig roast for a college graduation party.

"She was kind, she was funny, she was smart," recalled Michael Bruffee, a New York–based massage therapist who was in the midst of a three-month Buddhist retreat when we spoke and who in college was a Thurman Center regular and part of a slam poetry group with Ocasio-Cortez. "Everybody I knew was in love with her."

"We all loved her," recalled Adam Engel, who was a year behind Ocasio-Cortez at BU and also a regular at the Thurman Center. "She was very, very smart, very sweet, very welcoming. Just a good person. You have seen her on the news, and that is how she was in college. Passionate, outspoken, intelligent, engaging. Just fun to be around."

The Thurman Center was led by Kenneth Elmore, the dean of students at the school. After Ocasio-Cortez's election in 2018, he told a university newspaper that she was brought to the center by a friend who introduced her as "the smartest person I know," an assessment that Elmore came to agree with.[2]

"Sandy is brilliant—she is boldly curious and always present," he said at the time. "She makes me think and could always see multiple sides of any issue. Sandy is also heart and soul real. It is wonderful to see Sandy emerge as a leader—I can't wait to see what happens when her time truly comes."[3]

Engel, who went on to become a science teacher at a public school in Seattle, remembered sitting in Thurman Center until custodial staff would come in to close it, and then a few of the remaining students, Ocasio-Cortez often included, would go to a back room to talk further into the night until the group was kicked out of there too. Politics, campus gossip, and general adolescent silliness ruled the day.

"She was really a genuinely kind person," recalled Eric Calvin Baker, another fellow student and friend. "People ask me all the time when they find out that I was friends with her, 'Is it real? Is it an act?' And all I can tell them is that the person you see on TV is 100 percent her. And the thing I most remember about her and that drew me and others to her was that she just had this incredibly deep well of empathy, and this incredible ability to listen. I know people may scoff at it, but it is genuinely incredible. When you are talking with her, you feel like she is totally engaged with you. It is just this ability to make you feel seen and feel heard. I think it is one of the reasons she has become the leader of this movement. There is a strong energy about her that exudes kindness and empathy and says, 'I see you and I am going to fight for you,' and she always had that."

When conversations would get heated in the Thurman Center, as the group gathered on any given Friday and the conversation would get heated, it was Ocasio-Cortez who would cut through the din and get the last word.

"She just had this sense of gravity about her," Baker said. "Like when she was in the room and when she was talking people knew to be quiet. She wasn't mean or presumptuous about it or anything, but just sort of commanded the room. I guess you could call it a natural charisma."

"There is this Maya Angelou quote, 'People may forget what you say but they will never forget how you made them feel.' That's what I always think of about her," said Engel. "There was always this calm fury, or not fury really, but power to her words. She was the one at the end who would sort of invite everyone to reflect on what we had said, what we were doing and talking about, how the event unfolded before us."

During her junior year, Ocasio-Cortez studied abroad in Niger, working on a project on maternal healthcare. She visited people sick with typhoid in straw houses, talked to women about their birth control, learned how to surf sand, visited an orphanage, and kept a blog documenting her travels. There, she learned local languages that were taught in French, and expressed amazement at her surroundings and at the kindness of the people. It was an eye-opener for a young woman who had mostly traveled between Westchester and the Bronx, with the occasional trip home to Puerto Rico, and then to Boston, not least because of the conservative Islamic culture she encountered there.

In one blog post, she wrote:

> It is difficult to capture into words the role that women play in Niger. In fact it would be difficult to capture the role that any half of a population would play in a developing nation. The terms "feminism" and "empowerment" don't seem to capture the priorities of our generation, and the words themselves sound like relics from the past, frumpy and outdated. We no longer live in the same fight for equality of prior generations, we have moved to the widely accepted reality that marginalizing 50% of a given population doesn't make much sense, mathematically or socially. Enabling women to learn, create, and manage enterprises is not [a] discussion of feminism but rather a global strategy for development. . . .
>
> It is in this line of thought with which we approach the opportunities granted to women and their children, a clear departure from the "equality for equality's sake" struggles of the past. This is a time of forward movement, and because societies tend to be as strong as their weakest player, one must look towards the marginalized in order to progress.[4]

Ocasio-Cortez had arrived at Boston University hoping to study medicine, dreaming of becoming an OB-GYN. In Niger, a nation recovering from widespread famine, she did rotations at a maternity clinic in the capital city of Niamey. "I saw a lot of pretty brutal things there," she told *Bon Appétit* magazine. She saw babies born

on steel tables covered with nothing but thin cloth, and she wit-
nessed one stillbirth. "The reason the child had passed was very
preventable. For me it was a very powerful moment," she said. "This
child's life was literally decided because of where it was born."[5]

After Ocasio-Cortez returned to Boston University, school ad-
ministrators shut down the Niamey International Development
program after armed soldiers stormed the presidential palace in Niamey and captured President Mamadou Tandja and formed a ruling
junta. When the program was reinstated the following fall, Ocasio-
Cortez was quoted in the school newspaper as encouraging students
to participate in the program and urging the university to keep
it open.

"Nigeriens are an overwhelmingly peaceful people. Even with
the political instability that hung in the air, the most discomfort
that I felt was an uncertainty about the future of the Nigerian [sic]
people," Ocasio-Cortez said. "Our security was a high priority for
the U.S. Embassy and of our Nigerien friends and host families, and
I never doubted their abilities to take care of us."[6]

But if there was a moment that really changed Ocasio-Cortez's
life as a young person, and that set her on the path to politics, it
was her father dying at the beginning of her sophomore year. Sergio
Ocasio was just forty-nine years old when he died of lung cancer.

His story was in many ways the story of the American dream.
He grew up in the Bronx in the 1970s, back when it was one of the
most dangerous and burned-out places on earth. He got into Brooklyn Tech, and ultra-selective high school in New York City, and
spent over an hour commuting to school each day. He met AOC's
mother, Bianca Cortez, in Puerto Rico, where the two married before settling in the Bronx. They bought an apartment in the sprawling twelve-thousand-unit middle-income Parkchester complex
for $36,000 and later bought another similarly priced unit nearby,
where Ocasio kept an office for his small architectural practice.

His business, Kirschenbaum and Ocasio Roman Architects PC,
was a licensed minority-owned business with New York State, which

meant they were beneficiaries of a law designed to level the playing field when awarding state contracts. The firm mostly focused
on remodeling and renovations. Clients included the Parkchester
complex, where the Ocasio-Cortez family owned an apartment, as
well as other middle- and low-income housing developments and
not-for-profits.

Ocasio was not only the family's sole breadwinner but the lodestar
of young Alexandria's life, the person who pushed her, believed in
her, challenged her, and insisted that she learn about current events
and defend her position on the news of the day. As Ocasio-Cortez
said in the documentary *Knock Down the House*, when she was
around five years of age or so, her father went on a planned road trip
to Florida with some buddies of his, and Ocasio-Cortez begged to
tag along. Eventually he relented, and the gang stopped in Washington, DC, to get a look at the Capitol and the White House.

"He said, 'You know, this all belongs to us,'" she said. "'This is
our government, so all of this stuff is yours.'"

When her father lay dying, Ocasio-Cortez rushed home to see
him at the hospital. His last words to her were, "Make me proud."
Friends who knew her in Yorktown told me that while Ocasio-Cortez
was always serious, dedicated, and driven, they noticed a change
come over her after Sergio passed—she seemed to find a new purpose. As she tells it, she threw herself into her schoolwork and into
campus life at Boston University, scarcely giving herself time to
grieve.

While at BU, Ocasio-Cortez was part of a spoken word/slam poetry group called Speak for Yourself. Michael Bruffee still remembers, over ten years later, a poem she wrote about her father called
"The Topaz Cape of Courage."

"I remember it because she had a way with words. The pain that
she felt flowed so beautifully into that piece. She was painting her
father, and her relationship with her father, in this way that had
no pretentious bullshit," he recalls. "She talked about him dying,
and him being in the hospital, and he wrapping her in this topaz

cape of courage and said, 'Do me proud.' I asked her about the topaz, because I didn't know what it was, and she said it was this
semi-precious stone that is blue and kind of cracked. It was this
image of something that wasn't perfect, that said it was OK to be
broken, and courage is wearing that."

Bruffee had his own struggles in college, including a father suffering from Alzheimer's, and by his own admission Bruffee threw
himself into drink, drugs, and eventually Zen meditation. Ocasio-
Cortez, on the other hand, "just threw herself into her work and
said I am going to get this shit done."

Ocasio-Cortez developed a poetic and artistic sensibility in
college that would carry her through to her political career. Re-
calling a Coffee and Conversation meeting on his own Dean of
Students blog, Dean Elmore wrote, "We had one of those moments
last Friday. During our conversation about happiness, Alexandria
Ocasio-Cortez—we know her as Sandy—stopped us cold with this
poem," and then proceeded to quote the poem, called "Questions,"
in full. It was written just a few weeks before Ocasio-Cortez was
going to graduate, and it is the voice of a young woman unsure of
what she is supposed to do next in her life.

> *Where are we going?*
> *When birds sing to one another, are they looking for melody or harmony?*
> *I've never been the one with answers.*
> *How is it that our eyes betray us?*
> *What does tomorrow bring?*
> *Just questions. Enigmatic, urgent, smoldering questions.*
> *But this, this is a world of answers:*
> *where to go, what to do, how to get rich quick –*
> *the degree to make you slick*
> *the title you want to hit*
> *the right dosage for your sick.*
> *Well, I've forgotten about the ready-made bullets in that gun*
> *because for me, not knowing is half the fun*
> *It's the uncertain moment before a first kiss*

It's trying to remember if your seatbelt clicked
It's the ride.
And I don't really know about this world full of answers
But I think I'll hold on to my questions
Because if not knowing is half the fun
Then inventing the answers on a bed of dew drops is the other
I'll show you the color of my love
or at least I can try
but maybe in that case, two makes better than one.
I just ask that you leave your answers at home
because to be honest, I don't really care about where we're going.
I care about who we become along the way.

At the Thurman Center, Ocasio-Cortez and some of her class-mates started a blog called *Culture Shock*, which mostly featured personal essays and observations from regulars at the center. As editor of the blog, Ocasio-Cortez wrote the first post, which was addressed to the school's students, faculty, alumni, and fans.

"Welcome to the beginning of a new era," Ocasio-Cortez wrote. "Oftentimes we as a community become a little too entrenched in the daily grind. Wedged between busy schedules and overachiev-ing classmates are piles of work so high the Prudential Center itself looks up to them. The plunging depths of our to-do lists can easily snatch us from taking a pause and laughing at ourselves, but BU Culture Shock is here to help you out. We're going to point out campus fumbles, strange happenings, and oddly juxtaposed mo-ments throughout Boston University for your sanity."[7]

The posts could be mostly frivolous about parties and relation-ships on campus and gripes about the administration, but Ocasio-Cortez's were different. Consider the first couple of posts when the site went live. One was about a local pizzeria hosting a benefit. Other topics focused on hummus, sunbathing on the campus green, the band Outkast, and "Bros vs. Hipsters." Ocasio-Cortez instead wrote about Frida Kahlo. "With brush in hand, boasting her te-huana dress and strong brow, Frida Kahlo charged into the fray as a political, social, and artistic revolutionary. Kahlo stood as a living, breathing challenge to preconceived notions of class, morality, art, your breakfast, everything," Ocasio-Cortez wrote. "It's easy to see why. A single glance at one of her paintings makes one feel uncomfortable, vulnerable, and exposed. This is bizarre, considering most of Kahlo's works are self-portraits: Frida as a tree. Frida as a hunted deer. Frida, as fiery and unapologetic as her marriage to Diego Rivera," she added, going on to recommend recent fictionalized movies and books that told the story of the artist's life.[8]

Ocasio-Cortez wrote another post in which she railed against the kind of "conscious consumerism" that well-meaning people engage in in the hopes of assuaging their guilty capitalistic consciences. "We've made a world where 10% proceeds sprinkle karma on our transactions. Does that make us any closer to an altruistic society?" she wrote. "There is some credit in giving a remote cocoa farmer 0.1% of our cookie purchase; after all, it's something. Yet at the end of the day, we still avoid eye contact with the homeless. Is social consciousness enough? What about social action? Is donating money action enough?"

Friends say that she was animated in college by a lot of the same concerns that animated her early political career: immigration, an economic system that helped the working class get a leg up, the environment. "We used to joke, you know, 'Sandy for President,'" said Bruffee, "because she was a very radical person back then. Not in a fire-and-brimstone way but in a way that she wanted to shake things up and push things to the left. We would talk all the time, 'Why don't one of us run for office?' and we would talk about the things we would do, just wipe the slate clean and provide healthcare, education, eliminate student debt, end the wars. If we just wiped the slate and started clean, what would it look like?"

"Obviously, none of us knew what a democratic socialist was or anything like that," agreed Adam Engel. "But she was a very caring person. She cared for people whether she knew them or not, which is sort of what democratic socialism is in a way."

Mina Vahedi, who is also a teacher and who lived on Ocasio-Cortez's dorm freshman year—and who was the student who introduced her to the Thurman Center and Dean Elmore—told a university alumni news agency after Ocasio-Cortez's win that her friend "just has this energy that's so motivated and ready just to work and make things happen." She recalled walking through campus and joking with Ocasio-Cortez about what would happen "when you're president one day." "She didn't make it seem like it was totally out of the question," Vahedi recalled.

Most of her friends, though, didn't see politics in Ocasio-Cortez's future. They thought she would go into nonprofit work, likely something with education back in the Bronx or among the Latino community. Still, in 2007 and 2008, Barack Obama, despite running as a center-left candidate, captured the hearts of the Democratic Party and of young Democrats especially who were thrilled at the prospect of electing not just a brilliant orator with an equally brilliant mind but someone who seemed a harbinger of a new, diverse America, presenting the chance for the country to at last cleanse itself of its racialized past. In February of her freshman year, Ocasio-Cortez hopped on a bus, traveling from Boston to Yorktown and then back to Boston, just for the purpose of voting for Obama.

A few days before the New York Super Tuesday primary, Ted Kennedy shocked the political world by endorsing Obama, a pointed rebuke to Hillary Clinton. And that summer, Ocasio-Cortez would join Kennedy's office as an intern. The liberal lion of Massachusetts only had another year to live, and would spend it pushing for the cause that animated most of his career: universal healthcare for all Americans, something that would later propel Ocasio-Cortez's own run for office. Ocasio-Cortez was one of the few Spanish speakers in the office and worked for Kennedy's immigrant constituent office as the senator battled the Bush administration, which was ramping up immigration enforcement and stationing Immigration and Customs Enforcement agents outside of daycare centers to detain undocumented immigrants. Kennedy, along with fellow Massachusetts

senator John Kerry, pushed for guidelines from the Bush administration that would limit actions against single parents who were
primary caregivers facing deportation.[9] It was one of Kennedy's last
official acts before being diagnosed with brain cancer.

Most of Ocasio-Cortez's energy however was focused on campus,
not off. If you were a Boston University student at the end of the
first decade of the twenty-first century—even if you weren't a regular at the Thurman Center or part of the regular Coffee and Conversation group or in the slam poetry group or in Alianza Latina,
the school's Latin American student organization—you more than
likely knew who Alexandria Ocasio-Cortez was, even on a campus
of eighteen thousand undergraduate students.

She was part of what was known as "The BU 500," those prominent students who are not only in every extracurricular activity but
lead a handful of them, seem to have a close relationship with the
administration, and are quoted fairly often in the school newspaper.
She gave a Ted Talk alongside other Boston-area college students,
in which her bio read: "A social entrepreneur and New York native,
Alexandria seeks out partners in health, art, and economic development to create opportunities for the future. She has consulted
non-profits, worked in government, and launched a media enterprise aimed toward these ends." She was mentioned in a *Washington
Post* story about college journalism that mentioned *Culture Shock*
as "a record of campus art, fashion and culture."[10] She was quoted
in a National Public Radio story about how college students were
reacting to the killing of Osama bin Laden by US forces.[11] At a
moment when most of the rest of the country was out celebrating,
Ocasio-Cortez, who was given the last word in the piece, sounded
a note of caution, questioning American foreign policy in the war
on terror.

"Now that the story line is no longer as simple as Obama versus
Osama, senior Alexandria says young people will be putting a lot
more pressure on the president to justify a war that's costing them
friends and family," reporter Tovia Smith intoned, before handing

the microphone over to AOC, who said, "Now that this villain has been slayed, questions like what are we doing [in Afghanistan] may have less of an answer today than we did yesterday."

Ocasio-Cortez remained close to her Boston University community in the years after she graduated, traveling back for reunions and special events, hosting friends when they would come through New York City, and officiating at occasional weddings. But in many ways, Ocasio-Cortez's life after graduation was similar to that of other Millennials. It came to be called "the quarter-life crisis," named after a 2001 book by the same name that chronicled the difficulties twentysomethings face when they are thrust out of the structures and community of college life and find themselves struggling to make their way in a world that they were told was theirs for the taking.

Ocasio-Cortez graduated from college in 2011 and entered an economy that was still slowly recovering from the Great Recession of three years before. Her situation was different from that of many of her peers, however, because her father had passed away and the family was left to struggle while Ocasio-Cortez had tens of thousands of dollars in student loans to pay off.

After Ocasio-Cortez won election and achieved near overnight stardom on the basis of her biography—that of a Bronx girl turned bartender who made her way to Congress on the back of a fiercely progressive platform—conservatives tried to lie about her background, saying that her story was one of the American dream, not of deprivation. They pointed to the fact that she went to an elite college (ignoring that she got scholarships and took out student loans) and grew up not in the Bronx but in Westchester County, a prosperous suburb with a median income of around $90,000.

But Ocasio-Cortez was always quite explicit that the home in Yorktown Heights, a town of under two thousand people in Westchester County, was purchased with the help of aunts, uncles, and other relatives to give the Ocasio-Cortez children a better future and a better education than could be had in the Bronx.

That division, between the upper middle-class, upwardly mobile, and largely white surroundings of Yorktown Heights and the poor urban Black and Latino neighborhoods of the Bronx, was one that Ocasio-Cortez returned to frequently and where much of her extended family still lived. That forty-five-minute journey, between one of the richest counties in America and one of the poorest, became the rhetorical foundation of Ocasio-Cortez's political career. "I was born in a place where a zip code determines your destiny," she famously intoned in the viral ad that launched her campaign. People who knew her before her political career say it was something she talked about often, how in Westchester she was often the lone Latino in her class, while with family back in the Bronx she wasn't Latin enough.

"We both had this common experience of having Latino parents, at least one of whom was new to the country, leaving their zip code in order to have a better life for their kids," recalled Julio Cotto, who became close to Ocasio-Cortez in the years after college. "Your kids are now in this very kind of foreign upbringing where you are an outsider or you are now *really* a minority. Other kids in your family make fun of you because of the way you speak English, because you don't speak with an urban accent [or] with a Latino accent and on the other hand back home you are trying to win all the trophies to prove yourself. Alexandria's cousins were in the inner city and surrounded by the urban Latino and Puerto Rican culture, but she's getting to compete in science competitions and doesn't have to necessarily worry about her safety."

Cotto remembers Ocasio-Cortez telling a story about how she wanted to prove herself by selling the most Girl Scout cookies in her troop. She would work the doors of her neighborhood, seemingly getting more orders than everyone else around, but "then there were some Westchester County families that would just come and buy hundreds of cookies from their own kids. She couldn't catch a break."

One thing Yorktown was not was diverse. Jose Alvarado, a class-mate of hers, said that the two of them were the only Puerto Rican kids in their class. Another friend said there were only a handful of Asian kids in their class of three hundred, and no African American students.

"I remember being a senior in an AP government class and the teacher decided to debate immigration," Ocasio-Cortez recalled in an interview. "And this girl said Mexicans need to learn how to speak English. No, she actually said Mexicans need to learn how to speak American. And I turned and I looked at her, as if to say, 'Hello?' And she said, 'Oh, you're not one of those Mexicans.' And so growing up this was the dynamic that I had."

And even upper-class towns can have working- and middle-class enclaves, and that is very much the area that Ocasio-Cortez lived in. "Her house was very nice and comfortable and cozy, don't get me wrong, but believe me it was like a fifth of the size of the rest of our friend's houses," said one friend.

"I grew up in a town that was in retrospect much more con-servative than me," Ocasio-Cortez told me. "At a time when the American middle class was really shrinking. The financial crisis touched everybody in my neighborhood. And while my town was pretty affluent, I didn't grow up in a cul-de-sac or in a development or anything like that. My actual neighborhood was nurses, retirees, firefighters, police officers, teachers, jobs that are supposed to be solidly middle class, but since I was a kid have slipped and become working class and working poor."

The town as a whole, former classmates say, was a slice of Amer-icana, a place that hosted an annual fireman's carnival every sum-mer, a Christmas lights parade every winter, concerts in the park in June, and community theater at the local cultural center. It was a place where most of the graduating class of students went to col-lege, but many stayed local, attending either a State University of New York public college or another private alternative nearby. Most bounced around after college, often in New York City, before returning home to Yorktown Heights to start their own families.

Sandy was known in high school as being friendly and driven with a bit of a goofy streak, but also something of a nerd. As the hippies gathered outside for lunch and the jocks took over the cafeteria, Ocasio-Cortez and her friends would eat lunch in the science research room. She was in a two-and-a-half year science-intensive program and competed in multiple science fairs in her free time. Her awards included a Future of Medicine Award from the Westchester County Medical Society, a first place in the microbiology category at the Westchester Science and Engineering Fair, best in fair at the New York State Science and Engineering Fair, and a second place among over 1,500 entrants in the Intel International Science and Engineering Fair in Albuquerque, New Mexico, for identifying three chemical antioxidants that doubled the life span of a roundworm, an achievement that won her scholarship money, a mention on the NBC *Nightly News* and led to an asteroid being named after her since the judges of the competition were granted naming rights.[12]

"She was so good at that because she was such an effective communicator," recalled one friend. "She knew how to grab people's attention. I think everyone still remembers that Intel presentation. She just absolutely crushed it."

"She was amazing," one of her favorite teachers, Michael Blueglass, told a local Yorktown Heights news site in the hours after her election. "Aside from her winning one of the top spots and going to the [Intel International Science and Engineering Fair], she was just one of the most amazing presenters in all of the years I've been at Yorktown. Her ability to take complex information and explain it to all different levels of people was fantastic."

"She's always wanted to make a difference," he added. "She cares about other people tremendously, always did. She was always friendly with all different groups of students and she always cared about doing the right thing. Even if the easiest thing was not expedient, she would do whatever it took to help people."

Ocasio-Cortez's interest in science led her to getting involved, in a modest way, in local politics. The pond in front of her middle school was dirty, and so Ocasio-Cortez, then just twelve years old, went to investigate why with a group of friends. They discovered that the pond was not aerated and didn't have enough oxygen for anything to grow. Along with a teacher, the group went to the Yorkville town board to request an aerator.

"That was my first real experience with activism, making a presentation in front of all of these older people about why we need an aerator," Ocasio-Cortez said. "I don't even think we ever got the aerator, but I remember kind of making that pitch."

If there was another guiding force in Ocasio-Cortez's life it was a thirty-year-old nonprofit in Central Texas called the National Hispanic Institute (NHI), that was founded in the post–civil rights, post–Chicano activism era in order to prepare the country's growing Hispanic population for success in college, their careers, and leadership roles in their communities.

Ocasio-Cortez participated in NHI programming before her junior year in high school when she, along with 150 or so of her peers, went to the group's Lorenzo de Zavala Youth Legislative Session (LDZ). It operated something like a Model UN, as the teens made speeches and ran for different positions within the organization, trying to build coalitions and garner support from their fellow students. "LDZ gives you a platform to test out your ideas and opinions, while also gauging your own leadership strengths and growth potential among your peers," the program's materials state. "Colleges and universities will also be certain to recognize how as an LDZ student you carry that special star quality they look for in candidates who will become campus leaders."

"We use a mock government to teach kids to understand how to work within an organization, how to understand policy, how to understand constituency development, all of which to us are experiences that'll be beneficial to college, their career," said Julio Cotto, a director with the organization and a longtime friend of Ocasio-Cortez's. "And more importantly, if they choose to be civic and community leaders, we know that a lot of what can trip a leader up. It's just that kind of knowledge of understanding that organizations all have their own way of operating their own values, their own protocol."

At the summer institute, Ocasio-Cortez ran for every office available. This was high school, and so the election could be little more than a popularity contest, and the students would organize themselves into packs and trade favors or buy each other lunch for voters. Most of the students were from Chicago or Texas, and had some time with one another before arriving at the conclave, while Ocasio-Cortez was just one of two students from the East, and the only one from New York. She lost every election she ran for.

"I really floundered," she told NHI founder Ernesto Nieto in a podcast the two of them recorded together six weeks before Ocasio-Cortez won her surprise election.[13] "But I was really good at not getting discouraged. It's something present-day me could learn from fifteen-year-old me. I ran for so many things and I think I learned to adopt this attitude of, 'Well, this isn't working so let's adapt.' I was a babe in the woods with all of these kids coming in twenty kids deep from their high schools, and it was half naivete and half just an attitude of 'Screw it,' and so I just kind of dove in.

"Which, now that I think about it, is exactly how I would characterize my run for Congress right now," she added after a beat.

What Ocasio-Cortez didn't mention, however, was that by the end of the program, the students nominate each other for various awards, and Ocasio-Cortez was named "Most Promising Female" out of more than two hundred students, despite being new to the group.

One of the striking things about Ocasio-Cortez, and something that has surely led to her sudden stardom, is her preternatural sense of self-possession. For such a young woman thrust onto the national stage, she seemed remarkably comfortable in her own skin and aware in some deep and internal way of who she was and what she wanted to do. Despite having just turned twenty-seven years old when she started her run for Congress, she seemed to have emerged from a box as a fully formed candidate.

And it is easy to draw a straight line from that woman who appeared on the national stage in 2018 to the teenager who went to
the NHI summer program, where she learned the skills of a candidate—speechmaking, appealing for votes, building a coalition—
skills that few politicians ever get to practice in their youth.

"When I thought about running, I basically had to say, 'Okay,
well if I'm going to do this, I need to basically run like no one else
has ever run before in the State of New York," Ocasio-Cortez told
Nieto. "I really had to run in a way that was fully expressive of who
I am, and my campaign had to be that too. There's the challenge
of building power where no one has bothered to build power before. And we're doing it without corporate money, which is highly
unusual in New York City politics. I feel like I was always kind of
confused by the word 'navigate' because navigate implies finding
the right direction and I never know if what I am doing is the
'right' thing to do. But I just know that my choices are true to who
I am. And I found that NHI helped me so much in that because
NHI helped me develop who I am and be confident in who I am.
And I really learned that when I am trying to navigate by what I
think is 'right' by external standards, I almost never do well. But
when I navigate and make decisions based on what feels like the
right thing to do for me or the smart thing to do for me it usually
ends up well."

But NHI taught Ocasio-Cortez more than how to train as a
candidate and how to listen to her own internal standards. The
primary activity of the LDZ, which is running for office and forming
a government of sorts—all run by the "Secretary of State"—taught
Ocasio-Cortez, even as she ran and lost for office after office, that
politics is, in a way, a fiction, that power only exists because people
say it does.

"I really do see the power of the establishment as very much the
way the LDZ is constructed," said Ocasio-Cortez. "It's the Wizard
of Oz. You think about your Secretary of State, it's the ultimate
allegory because the only thing that gives this thing the illusion of
power is the fact that we just believe that it's powerful. But in truth,

they could have no power at all. And that is ultimately the fear that [the political establishment] has. It's an emperor with no clothes situation. They're afraid that Toto is gonna rip back that curtain and they're going to find out that it's just some dude on a machine."

NHI wanted its students to focus on seeing the whole system and not just to tinker around the edges or fiddle here and there but to come up with entirely new paradigms.

"The NHI philosophy is that if you're a leader, we would rather you try to figure out ways to harness, invest resources, create new opportunities, new products, new organizations as opposed to reforming or just assimilating to the mainstream," said Cotto. "So, one of the things that our kids get challenged a lot on is that if you propose something that's pretty mainstream—like, say someone proposed doubling the funding for charter schools—our response is, okay, well that's within the context of mainstream. That's not really even original. It's not bad. But think of something else, something different, something new. To be a leader, you need to think of a 360-degree approach. And our founder, coming out of the civil rights movement, realized at some point you can only sustain negativity for so long, you can only sustain an 'anti-this, we've been wronged, this is an injustice' kind of thing for so long.

"But if you can inspire and if you can motivate people through something that's new, that's a positive. So if I, as a Latino leader, spend a lot of my time talking about things that need fixing, it just reinforces the deficiency or the narrative of deficiency as opposed to talking about investment and identifying all of the value that is within the community and finding ways to monetize it or to harness it or to turn it into different types of capital. That would be more in the spirit of the institute."

Ocasio-Cortez acknowledged taking these concepts to heart in her campaign, and they have played out in her political career. After all, what was the Green New Deal, which was the signature policy idea of Ocasio-Cortez's first term, if not a way of reconceptualizing an issue in a way that overturned the existing paradigm? Policies that will help the environment are often described as necessarily hurting the economy, but the Green New Deal subverts this framework, pitting economic growth and environmental sustainability as necessarily related.

"The big way that we mobilize people is saying that things can be different for us and the future can be ours if we believe that we can make it happen," Ocasio-Cortez said. "So you've got elements proceeding only on faith there, but what we do is exactly what NHI teaches us to do, which is to paint a picture and have the vision for the community as to what we can accomplish together. And then use that as the emotional, spiritual, political rallying point to organize individuals to take control of their collective destiny."

The NHI wasn't just something that Ocasio-Cortez did a couple of summers while she was in high school. It's how she got connected to Boston University, which was actively recruiting among NHI students when Ocasio-Cortez was in high school. During college and after, she returned to work at the institute in various capacities, and when she refers to herself as "an educator" in her campaign materials, she is referring to her time leading students at NHI.

Ocasio-Cortez wrote the afterword to Nieto's memoir, *Third Reality Revealed: Vision, Persistence, and Inventing a New Latino Identity* when she was still in college.

"How does the world begin anew?" Ocasio-Cortez wrote in what was more a prose poem than a typical afterword. "The question swirls in our minds, driven by a desire to venture and a penchant for gain. It clicks at our ears, rattling our fears of mediocrity and shaking us from our slumber. It eats at our food and steals its taste until our ultimate discovery: we are the builders."

"We are the builders, the bringers of the world to come," she continued. "Our memories are filled with smooth mud brick and scrolls of our visions. We cast iron for ourselves and carve ebony for our families. We raise schools for our teachers and homes for our children. The fruits of our labor bring bread to our baskets. But we must choose what we build."

After graduation, AOC returned to NHI as a social entrepreneurship fellow and then, a couple of years after that, as a faculty trainer. She worked several summers in a program called the Collegiate World Series and even took a week off from the campaign in 2018 to lead one of the institute's seminars.

People who were with her at NHI remember her as not just warm and ambitious but as unusually open about what she wanted. When the program's leaders looked for students to return the next year as organizers, others maneuvered to get noticed, but Ocasio-Cortez just went up to the program leaders and said she wanted to be included. That kind of initiative was what the program hoped to foster among a population of young people who often don't get that kind of encouragement.

"We give kids a chance to taste success and to taste challenges and even failure, but in a healthy, culturally safe way, which they wouldn't get otherwise. So when kids confront things later on in their life, they aren't facing it for the first time," said Cotto. "I remember when I would go into a government office, or have to go meet a university official there wasn't a fear factor because NHI had put me in capitol buildings since I was sixteen years old. I at least knew how to fake it."

And through NHI Ocasio-Cortez learned how to command a room, especially when she went back as a paid trainer in college and afterward, working with students who were not much older than she was. People who knew her then and in college describe her as dreamy, quiet, and introverted. She was obsessed with art, books, and ideas, a devoted fan of the writer David Foster Wallace, pushing his essay, "Consider the Lobster," in which he explores the ethics of killing animals of any sort for food, upon anyone who would take it. Her friends also describe her as insisting on taking detours on road trips if there was a Frank Lloyd Wright building to be seen.

But leading large groups of kids in a king-of-the-mountain parliamentary live-action role-play brought out in Ocasio-Cortez the ability to speak in such a way that would force people to listen. "You had to be very powerful," said Tanya Fernandez-Alaniz, who ran workshops with Ocasio-Cortez at NHI and is now an immigration attorney in Houston. "You had to portray confidence. You had to command a room. You could tell she was thoughtful and intelligent, but when it was time to be on stage, she was on. She was the same person I see now."

As Ocasio-Cortez bounced around in her college years, she had what was essentially a standing offer to return to NHI and work full-time. But Ocasio-Cortez yearned to return home.

"That was one thing that stood out about her," Cotto said. "She took the community concept a bit further than the others. It wasn't about helping her career or building a network. She wanted to be inside her actual community, living there, engaging it from the roots. A lot of our kids talk about it, but she actually did it, which was rare. She had been in and out of schools in the Bronx and saw some things she didn't like, and I think she knew she needed to be with her community and with her family."

Ocasio-Cortez settled in New York, became an amateur photographer and became a member of an Art Space in Queens, started regularly blogging, applied for work in the field of international development, and, when that went nowhere, got more and more interested in the city's burgeoning tech scene. She was interested in how to do good in a winner-take-all economy without dropping out entirely. She started a publishing company called Brook Avenue Press, which was designed to produce books and educational materials that gave a positive impression of the Bronx and the greater Latino community.

"What Brook Avenue Press seeks to do is help develop and identify stories and literature in urban areas," Ocasio-Cortez said in a promotional video about the project in 2011, soon after she graduated from BU. "And so really what we try to find is designers, artists, authors that really know the urban story and help develop stories for kids to expand their world for them."

She attended a press conference with US senator Kirsten Gillibrand in the Bronx for a bill called the Small Business Start-Up Support Act, which Gillibrand said would help tech start-ups by increasing the amount they could deduct in business expenses from $5,000 to $10,000.

"And Alexandria Ocasio-Cortez, 22, has shelled out $1,000 since April simply to rent space while she researches her business idea—a children's book publishing company devoted to telling positive stories set in The Bronx," read a local news story on the press conference, which included a quote by her about her struggles as a would-be entrepreneur: "You don't really make a profit in your first year. To get taxed on top of that is a real whammy."[14]

Ocasio-Cortez found an office in a Bronx coworking space and, while there, met its founder, Cheni Yerushalmi, who had lobbied the city's Economic Development Corporation to invest in tech incubators in the Bronx as a response to the financial crisis of 2008.

Yerushalmi got an idea to start a company that would use LinkedIn to help colleges best leverage their alumni in order to help recent graduates get a job. He hired Ocasio-Cortez, whose role was to work with individual students to help them craft an online image to attract potential employers. "We spent hours together every day, and everything you see about her now was apparent then," said Yerushalmi, "She was a great writer. Smart. Cool. She had a great personality, and she sort of stuck out wherever she went. People knew she was in the room."

As they plotted business strategy, Ocasio-Cortez would quote her architect father—"measure twice, cut once"—but she largely didn't catch the entrepreneurial bug, and the company, called GAGEis, Inc., turned out to be a bust. They got one client, Monroe College in the Bronx, according to Yerushalmi. Other schools were uninterested.

Ocasio-Cortez had put aside the Brook Avenue Press idea to work for the start-up, but the pay was minimal, even for fresh-out-of-college standards. "We all kind of got disenchanted at the end," said Yerushalmi. "Money was tight. I know that she struggled, and it didn't help that I wasn't paying her much. I saw great things in her, and I told her as much, but she just wasn't a start-up person. It is not who she was."

Ocasio-Cortez went back to Boston during this time to give a speech alongside other recent alumni at a day-long conference about how to "tackle social changes through innovation," according to the conference program. Her speech was called "Why We Can't Wait" and was dedicated to "the role of youth in the Civil Rights and other social change movements." Ocasio-Cortez told "stories from her work in the South Bronx and [explored] current trends to identify what we can do together to contribute toward a better world."

"Her primary interests," the program continued, "lie in entrepreneurship and developing innovative, healthy, enterprising communities for generations to come."

After a year or so, GAGEis shut down, and Ocasio-Cortez's mother found herself in difficult financial straits as well. Ocasio-Cortez took up work in the service industry, working at a pair of restaurants and bars in the chic Union Square area of Manhattan. It was a dispiriting time. The pay was good, but the work was grimy, the customers gross, and the bosses seemingly no better; at one point, they lined up the staff at the Coffee Shop and ranked them by attractiveness, something that led Ocasio-Cortez to nearly quit.

"My experience as a waitress was very radicalizing," Ocasio-Cortez said in an interview. "Barack Obama talked about working at Baskin-Robbins for a summer as a teenager. This is not the same thing. I worked in restaurants for several years in my twenties. I was in and out of health insurance, paid cash for my medicine and my doctor's visits."

She would pay for doctor's visits with a stack of ones from tips she received opening beers at the bar, at one point burying her face in her hands and crying in a doctor's office because she didn't have the three hundred dollars for a blood panel. She was running for Congress at that point and waited all day at a public clinic, canceling campaign events.

"I was just sitting there with all of these families and I came to realize that the system was just fundamentally broken. It didn't need tinkering or fixes, it was just broken," she told me. "Restaurants are an inherently extraordinarily political environment. People don't really realize it, but it's a crucible of politics.

"People who are most vulnerable or people who fall through the cracks pick up restaurant shifts. It's undocumented busboys. It's everyone who has some crazy story. Most of them had lost a parent when they were younger than I had. There were people who had been pursuing a profession but working part time or trying to break into an industry. And once you are in that position, it's very, very hard to get out because the same way compound interest works for the rich, compound adversity works for working people, because now you don't have insurance, now you need to pick up an extra shift to go to the doctor, now you have less time to try to get an internship and so on."

It was eye-opening, and a lot to take on. Although Ocasio-Cortez lived between two worlds growing up, she had also gone to a very good college, as had most of her friends, even her friends from high school. She had been an entrepreneur and an educator. She was someone who had been a star in high school, a star in college, and a star as a graduate, who suddenly, through the vagaries of the modern economy, found herself serving overprivileged hipsters and overripe tourists.

"Here was this person who everywhere she had gone in her life—in high school, at BU, at NHI, had been recognized for her talents and valued for what she had to say," said Cotto. "And here she is working in a space where there isn't a lot of growth and there isn't a lot of learning."

"I felt a lot of despair," Ocasio-Cortez recalled. It wasn't just that her career had stalled out, although there was that too. "It wasn't long ago that we felt our lives were over; that there were only so many do-overs until it was just too late, or too much to take, or we were too spiritually spent," AOC wrote in an Instagram post accompanying her swearing-in with Nancy Pelosi.

"I was scrubbing tables + scooping candle wax after restaurant shifts & falling asleep on the subway ride home. I once got pick-pocketed, & everything I earned that day was stolen. That day I locked myself in a room and cried deep: I had nothing left to give, or to be. And that's when I started over. I honestly thought as a 28 year old waitress I was too late; that the train of my fulfilled potential had left the station."

Ocasio-Cortez was a member of a sixty-thousand-person group called Ladies Get Paid, a career development platform designed to help women at various stages of their careers learn from each other. Members are invited to participate in a private Slack channel, and there are town halls, conferences, career coaching, and workshops. Ocasio-Cortez attended the second one ever offered, on how to get unstuck in your career, and at a "Reinvention" town hall a year later, stood up and told the audience that she had always wanted to run for office, "but people who look like me, people who are like me, where I come from, don't do it."[15] She went to see life coach Megan Hellerer, who works with older millennial women who are "underfulfilled overachievers."

According to a profile in *New York* magazine, "Hellerer counseled her in the virtues of 'directional versus destinational thinking. . . . ' On a road trip, instead of picking a place to end up, pick merely east or west. Instead of hitting goals, think of 'warmer or colder' steps. Warmer, for Ocasio-Cortez, was going to community board meetings. Then it was volunteering for the 2016 Bernie Sanders campaign and taking time off work to go to Flint, Michigan, and then Standing Rock Indian Reservation, and after that getting the call from the PAC Brand New Congress, which would ask her to run for the NY-14 congressional seat."

"Even when she decided to run for Congress, she wasn't like, 'I'm going to win!'" Hellerer told the magazine. "And that's where the courage comes in. If she was like, 'I'm only taking a next step if I'm positive that this is going to be my career for the rest of my life'—you don't run for Congress in those circumstances, against [Joe] Crowley and all that."

Later, Ocasio-Cortez wrote on Instagram of Hellerer's advice: "Your guidance, help, and support was pivotal, in a time when I felt very lost. You helped me reframe a lot of my thinking and were part of a series of events that culminated in the big adventure of a Congressional run . . . and win!"

But Ocasio-Cortez's despair was political too.

She had enthusiastically supported Barack Obama, but at one point looked up who was the largest contributor to America's political campaigns, and saw that Goldman Sachs was a top contributor to both Republicans and Democrats. There were the extension of the Bush tax cuts, efforts to rein in Medicare and Social Security, and the drone warfare program abroad.

"I went through a phase where I kind of checked out," Ocasio-Cortez said. "It was like an experience similar to heartbreak. You go through enough bad relationships, then you say, 'Men are canceled' or 'I'm done with women.' And I went through that with politics. What is the point? And I can tell you, having that feeling, it doesn't feel good."

CHAPTER 2

THE DISTRICT

"Are all of the apartments smoking weed?" Alexandria Ocasio-Cortez asked. We were walking down the hallways of the Elmback apartments in Queens, a mostly working-class area on the other side of the elevated train line, and around the corner from Ocasio-Cortez's campaign headquarters. It was late June 2018, four days from the election, and Ocasio-Cortez's campaign was everywhere in Queens and the Bronx that summer and spring. Her posters, featuring her face staring off in the distance, with their comic-book-style blue-and-gold lettering and design, were ubiquitous in bodegas, dry cleaners, hipster bars, and chichi tchotchke shops, especially in the district's whiter, gentrified sections in western Queens.

The race was considered the longest of long shots. Her opponent, Joe Crowley, was not just the head of the powerful Queens County Democratic Party but someone who would-be governors, senators, and mayors came to on bended knee for an endorsement in the belief that such a nod came with a standing army of political foot soldiers. Plus, he was the fourth-highest-ranking Democrat in the House of Representatives, and the three people above him—Nancy Pelosi of California, Maryland's Steny Hoyer, and Jim Clyburn of South Carolina—were all in their late seventies.

Crowley was a comparatively sprightly fifty-five and known as one of the most popular politicians of either party in Congress, a hail-fellow well-met back-slapping Irish American pol who had been traveling around the country and raising money for his fellow Democrats to boost his bid to become the next Speaker of the House when the Democrats retook control the next year.

Crowley's team was well aware of the example of Virginia congressman Eric Cantor, who held Crowley's position on the Republican side in 2014 before losing to a little-known challenger, Dave Brat, in an upset that shocked the political world but that led to guffaws when it was revealed that Cantor had spent election day making fundraising calls from a DC-area Starbucks. Crowley's polling had him up over thirty points, and his team was certain he would win. They didn't know quite what to make of this young Latina from the Bronx, who called herself a "democratic socialist" and who was relentless in tagging Crowley as an out-of-touch carpetbagger (he lived most of the year with his family in northern Virginia). Crowley's family had been involved in Queens politics for a generation, and he came of age when it was more associated with Archie Bunker than as "The World's Borough" it would become in the first decades of the twenty-first century. By 2018, Queens was one of the most ethnically and linguistically diverse places on earth, and New York's Fourteenth Congressional District was 50 percent Hispanic and only less than 20 percent non-Hispanic white.

Crowley had come of age in the 1990s, when the Democratic Party moved to the right after a series of landslide losses at the presidential level. Crowley was a proud New Democrat, a congressional coalition who thought that the party should be more welcoming to Wall Street and more concerned with keeping taxes and spending low. He did not speak Spanish, and took to campaigning in the waning days of the race alongside Luis Gutiérrez, a retiring congressman from Chicago who could speak Spanish to Crowley's constituents.

In the Elmback apartments, meanwhile, Ocasio-Cortez asked me and another young aide, Daniel Bonthius, to stand aside when she knocked on doors so that residents wouldn't see two white guys flanking their entrance when they looked out through the peephole. It was the middle of the day on a Friday, so most residents who were home were the elderly and the semi-employed. Many didn't speak English, and when they didn't, Ocasio-Cortez spoke to them in Spanish. Many weren't registered to vote, and so she showed them how. Many didn't have citizenship or green cards, and she helped them with that too.

"What we're trying to do really is expand the electorate, educate the electorate," Ocasio-Cortez said as she went door to door. "This district has about three percent turnout [for congressional elections]. So when you can go to Congress with less votes than a city council race, you can really make big changes by changing who votes. It's a heavier lift, but what's different between the New York machine and, for example, the Chicago machine is that the Chicago machine has really built a strong voter turnout operation, and the New York machine really depends on voter suppression. It's not like they have a huge base of buildings and buildings of people who are super loyal."

Ocasio-Cortez knew the odds that she would win were almost impossibly long, but she said her race was about more than just winning.

"There's a secondary mission of organizing this community as I run," she said. "A lot of times if someone wanted to register to vote, canvassers would say, 'Google it,' and then they would go on to the next door. But for us, seeing someone like that is a win. We want to register that person right now. It's about something much bigger than just one election."

Talking to Ocasio-Cortez, it was hard not to be convinced that she could make it, despite what the pundits said about her chances. Ocasio-Cortez pounced on the questions I asked, laid out her case, and savaged her opponent for being a congressman too cozy with the financial industry and corporate lobbyists. She said Crowley should stay in northern Virginia, where he kept a home, and run for Congress from there rather than run for the seat in the Bronx and Queens he had served for twenty years. But still: hotshot challengers seemed to run every two years or so in New York, get a lot of media attention, and end up losing in a blowout. Why would this time be any different?

"What I think makes our campaign legitimately different is that we're actually organizing, and I can tell you that a lot of those other campaigns weren't," Ocasio-Cortez said. "Those folks were not do-ing the work. They were not knocking doors. And I know for a fact that we are."

I knew that if she won, it would be one of the greatest upsets in US political history and that Ocasio-Cortez would immediately become a star and hero of the Trump resistance.

"I think I'm ready for it," she said three days before she would go to bed obscure for the last time in her life. "And I think the country is ready for it."

Ocasio-Cortez could not have known, but when she decided to run for Congress in 2018, she was entering fertile territory, a district ripe for a revolution. The first nearly two decades of the twenty-first century had seen New York City recover from 9/11 and the finan-cial crisis to resume its position as a global capital, a place sucking in more and more of the country's brightest and most ambitious people. Median home prices in New York City had climbed 28.5 percent in the seven years before Ocasio-Cortez's election.[1] People had flocked to New York for jobs in technology, media, and the arts only to find themselves priced out of Manhattan and then priced out of Brooklyn, with some of them, at least, ending up in western Queens. They were rich by many standards, but they were still on the outside looking in at the increasingly gilded pleasure palace of New York City. They were ripe, in other words, for radical politics, just as Ocasio-Cortez was arriving on the scene.

Shawna Morlock was in many ways typical of the new kind of resident in the district. She was thirty-seven, a mother and a hair-dresser and colorist at a hip salon in SoHo who had bounced around Florida and Texas before settling in western Queens when her hus-band got a job in New York.

She was never much of an activist, but she followed politics fairly closely and would occasionally donate to candidates she cared about, like Bernie Sanders. The Women's March in January 2017, the day after Donald Trump's inauguration, was the first protest she had ever participated in.

Soon afterward, she saw a Facebook photo of a group of organizers canvassing the neighborhood with a quote from Ocasio-Cortez pasted over it: "Women like me aren't supposed to run for office." Here was a twentysomething working-class woman who talked about inequality, who wanted to get money out of politics, and who seemed as little like a politician as one could imagine.

"I felt like I had never really been represented by anyone in my whole life in a way, and everything she was saying was exactly what I would want in my representative," Morlock said.

She brought her five-year-old along to canvass with her—the first time she'd gone out knocking doors in the neighborhood—and was surprised to find the candidate herself there.

"AOC just exuded a genuine normality," Morlock said. "She didn't seem like a greasy, polished politician. You can feel it. She was a bartender, and I was too, for thirteen years, and you get to be a good judge of people's character in that position."

Out on the trail that day, Ocasio-Cortez told voters that she could deal with Donald Trump because as a bartender, "I have dealt with a hundred Donald Trumps."

"I was like, 'Yea! Me too, girl!'" recalled Morlock. "I know Trump doesn't even drink, but he's just like every rich guy at the bar who has had too much to drink and gets obnoxious and sloppy and doesn't realize people are trying to avoid him."

Ocasio-Cortez went to the Women's March too, wearing her father's Movado watch. She posted on Facebook about what that meant:

He was the first feminist I ever knew, and constantly reminded me that I had the power to control my own destiny. If he were here today, I know he would have dropped whatever he was doing to march with me. When I was 9 years old, I ran to my dad when a man on TV argued that women should primarily bear children and support the home. He listened, then turned to me and asked,

"Well, why shouldn't they?" It kicked me off balance, because I expected him to fight for me; tell me that the TV man was wrong. But instead, he made me articulate an argument and figure out how to stand up for myself and all people. He helped me find my voice, and then he amplified it.

Thank you to all the men who joined the Women's March in solidarity today. We see you by our side. And we love you for it.[2]

The Women's March was by some accounts the largest one-day protest in US history, with an estimated four million people marching, or roughly slightly more than 1 percent of the country's population. It began in the hours after Trump's election, in response to the Facebook post of a retired attorney and grandmother of four living in Maui, Hawaii, about the need for a march on Washington, DC, to protest the new president. The idea exploded as women around the country talked about marching to affirm the country's values and to stand up for all those who the president-elect had "insulted, demonized, and threatened" during the campaign: "immigrants of all statuses, Muslims and those of diverse religious faiths, people who identify as LGBTQIA, Native people, Black and Brown people, people with disabilities, survivors of sexual assault."[3]

The early promise of the Women's March as a movement collapsed under the weight of infighting and allegations of anti-Semitism among the march's leaders. But Ocasio-Cortez traveled to the march after returning to New York from the Dakota Access Pipeline protest on the Standing Rock reservation with her friend Maria Swisher. The two sat at a rest stop midway between New York and DC, one full of other people heading to the march, even though it was nearly one o'clock in the morning.

"It's an important moment. I feel we are at a really unique place in history," Ocasio-Cortez said as they sat in the darkness. "And when I think about things that I want to tell my kids that I did, this is it. This is the essence of what democracy should be about. This is everyday people. We aren't special, but what we are doing together is very special."

Ocasio-Cortez treated the Women's March like it was a media event—which, to be fair, it was—and she was a reporter covering it. Armed with a selfie-stick, she and Swisher livestreamed the march, answered viewer questions, and interviewed fellow marchers, including children. (Throughout the campaign, Crowley's team believed that Ocasio-Cortez was really auditioning for a position on *The Young Turks*, a left-wing opinion show on YouTube.) Afterward, on their way back to New York, Ocasio-Cortez and Swisher visited the Jefferson Memorial at one end of the National Mall. "Thomas Jefferson is one of my all-time favorite presidents. Lincoln is my all-time bae for sure, but as a writer and a philosopher it is pretty hard to compare anyone to Jefferson," Ocasio-Cortez said as she read some of Jefferson's quotes on the wall.

Someone shared on their feed with an apocryphal Jefferson quote about fear as a mechanism to control people and then commented: "I reached a point in my life . . . where I said I'm not going to make decisions based out of fear anymore. . . . Because fear I think is an inherently reactionary emotion. And I refuse to have my life led by reaction anymore. I'm going to have it led by courage. And courage is seeing what you want the world to look like and making your life bend to that, and it's not easy to do."

Two days after they returned to New York, a local state senator named Jose Peralta announced that he was leaving the Democratic Party to join a breakaway coalition of fellow Democratic state senators who caucused with the Republicans, a move that put the GOP in power in one chamber of the state capitol and gave the party, whose voters were outnumbered two to one in the state, the ability to stifle legislation that would have aided undocumented immigrants, boosted funding to city schools, and protected a woman's right to choose.

Albany remained opaque to even the most politically engaged New Yorkers, but it was clear, in the eyes of many, that a local representative had sided with the Trump administration just as a good portion of the country was consumed by fear.

The caucus that Peralta joined was called the Independent Democratic Conference (IDC), and it began on the very first day of the Governor Andrew Cuomo administration, leading many observers to suspect that Cuomo was secretly propping up the group in order to avoid being pulled too far to the left.

Activists had been organizing against the IDC ever since it was formed but had not caused much of a stir. The size of the IDC had waxed and waned over the years, but in the age of Trump, people with even a passing interest in politics came to realize that the system had broken down long before Trump.

In the Jackson Heights section of Queens, a neighborhood that was home to scores of recent immigrants but also to many young middle-class families looking for a place to raise their children, a local listserv, mostly reserved for parents to share neighborhood tips about family-friendly restaurants and nanny recommendations, was suddenly burning up with news of the elected official's betrayal.

"He'd better make a statement to us about this within the next 24 hours with great reasons why this serves his constituents," wrote one neighborhood mom. "Otherwise he's over."

"Called his office and communicated that democracy isn't something that only happens once every four years," wrote another neighborhood dad.

"I was trying to figure out what to do," said Susan Kang, a professor of political science at John Jay College in Manhattan. She had done a little bit of volunteering for Bernie Sanders in the 2016 primary but had just given birth to her second son and had a lot less time on her hands. "I was trying to figure out how to get appropriately involved. I just didn't know what to do. There were rallies all over about how to resist Donald Trump, and we would go with our babies and it would be freezing cold and we would march and get sick, and it all just seemed really futile," she said. "It was great for us emotionally but was shit in terms of being effective. It started to seem like a waste of time."

But when someone who lived around the corner seemed to be aligning with the Republicans, it was different. Kang, who didn't know what the IDC was before Peralta joined it, did a quick Google search and was appalled. She, along with a group of other neighborhood parents, began bombarding Peralta's office with phone calls, demanding a community meeting.

"At one point Peralta called me and he tried to butter me up. 'Oh hey. I was wondering, instead of a public thing, do you think maybe we could have a gathering at your house of your friends who are upset about this?' And I laughed at him. 'I'm not going to give you my house to do your job. Are you joking?' He said he was worried about troublemakers who may come from Brooklyn or something and I told him it's his job to answer to the public. 'What are you? You can't deal with angry feelings?' I was really mean to him, and I was not having it."

Peralta eventually relented, and a few weeks later he hosted a town hall in the neighborhood but didn't publicize it at all. So Kang blasted out the meeting on social media and flooded the neighborhood with signs and stickers promoting it. New neighborhood activist groups, like Hearts Across Queens, Astoria March, and Sunnyside Woodside Action Group, had sprung up in the days after Trump's election, and Kang began to reach out. The town hall, which was with an obscure state lawmaker who almost no one had heard of a few weeks before, was filled to capacity at a local community center, with locals lining up for hours ahead of time to get in.

It proceeded, predictably, with Peralta trying to make his case while overcoming boos and heckling from the audience. Kang livestreamed the whole affair on Facebook and sent it to a *New York Times* reporter, who wrote a piece on the ensuing circus, and the next week met up with two other activists who came up with the idea of No IDC NY, a group that would raise money and recruit progressive candidates to run against the other turncoat Democrats.

"We did what organizers generally do," Kang said. "We knew people who could do stuff for candidates. We took pictures of them before they had any money so they would have head shots, and we linked up volunteers to help them with their own web pages. We had dual fundraisers. We were in the community."

The group traveled to Albany to hold a mock jazz funeral for all the bills that had died due to the IDC's alliance with the GOP. Kang wore a black dress and carried a black umbrella. Each bill that died was represented by a mock tombstone. A bunch of musician activists provided the soundtrack.

The group ended up getting behind eight primary challengers from around the state; six won and gave Democrats control of both chambers in the state capitol. New York has byzantine election laws that are mostly designed to protect incumbents. One of the laws, since overturned, put the congressional primary and the state legislative and statewide primaries on separate days at the beginning and the end of the summer, and so AOC won her race three months before the No IDC candidates won theirs. But the fact that they had been organizing across the city, and especially in the Bronx and Queens, helped organize those neighborhoods when she appeared on the ballot.

"A lot of people here, they are new to the community, they are transplants. They fit my demographic profile, like they moved in from Brooklyn, but they are probably not from New York City. They are probably professional managerial class, but they have politics that are more progressive than the Democratic mainstream," said Kang. "And so NO IDC was sort of like an opening moment for them. If you were a newly angry mobilized activist who is a Democrat, what would you do? You go to your local Democratic club and you just fall asleep, right? It's boring. There are a bunch of seventy-five-year-olds who don't know how to use email. You go to the community board meeting, and it's a bunch of people fighting about street parking. That doesn't speak to you and what you want to do.

"Whereas you'll find people that you like at one of these new institutions. People who might share your passions. They share your concerns about Trump. They share your concerns about climate change. They share your concerns about raising children. And they're not part of the political establishment, and so they create almost like alternative machines, and by machines meaning ways of mobilizing volunteers and voters that emerged as a result of Trump, and they are independent of the establishment and they're new to the community."

While the anti-IDC organizing was getting underway, Ocasio-Cortez was officially becoming a candidate for Congress. One of the first things she did was knock on the doors of Republicans and unregistered and unaffiliated voters. The reason, again, was New York election laws that actually made it harder for its citizens to vote by requiring people who wanted to vote in a primary to change their registration nearly a year in advance (the law has since been changed). It had a limited effect on her final vote totals, surely, but it showed what a forward-thinking operation she was running.

A few months after she kicked off her campaign, Ocasio-Cortez showed up at a rally at a public park in the Forest Hills section of Queens, which was outside of her district. The rally, called "Queens Stand Up," was organized by a local labor lawyer. A number of groups—old (like the local chapter of the Communication Workers of America and the Council on Islamic-American Relations) and new (like Muslims for Progress, Black Lives Matter of Greater NY, No IDC NY, and NY Indivisible)—had organized it to "come together for liberty and our democracy in this uncertain time," calling the rally "our opportunity to stand up for American values."

It was a scorching hot June day, and Vigie Ramos Rios, a member of the Democratic Socialists of America (DSA), was there distributing information on behalf of her organization, when Ocasio-Cortez showed up, wearing a black dress, heels, and a blazer and got up on the small stage with a janky microphone.

Ramos Rios recalled that the rally was held at a shopping area with people passing through, but when Ocasio-Cortez spoke, some people stopped and actually listened to what she was saying. Ramos Rios went up to her afterward, gave Ocasio-Cortez her card, and told her, "If there is anything I can do, please let me know."

A few months later, Ramos Rios was hired as Ocasio-Cortez's campaign manager.

One of the organizers of the Queens Stand Up rally was Naureen Akhter, founder of Muslims for Progress. She was a stay-at-home mom and recipe blogger who ran to JFK airport to protest after Trump announced his Muslim ban. Afterward, she got together with a few fellow Bangladeshi Americans to fortify their community against an unknown threat stemming from the White House. She had tried to get involved with the local party organization, which Joe Crowley was in charge of, but found no point of entry: there was no website, no person to contact, and no schedule of meetings—for neither the county Democratic Party nor the myriad Democratic clubs in the county.

"A lot of us had big networks of friends and family, and we wanted to start tapping into that network and reeducating each other about policies and about our elected officials about whether they were voting in our favor. We wanted to start the conversation about the importance of voting as a block to really assert our community," Akhter told me.

There were other Muslim groups, including the Muslim Democratic Club of New York, that would hold meetings in the neighborhood, but, Akhter felt, "they were very seasoned, political operative types. A lot of them had roles in various elected officials' offices, and so they kind of had an ethos and paradigm that they were working around, and it wasn't what I was looking for. It felt a bit disconnected from what I was trying to do in terms of educating and mobilizing the immediate community out here in Queens."

Akhter remembers how Ocasio-Cortez wasn't on the roster of people to speak but that she showed up anyway, waiting on the side until asking the organizers if she could have a turn to speak. "She came out guns blazing. She was saying what I felt every Democrat needed to be saying—Medicare for All, just really bold, visionary ideas. Things that were really animating and energizing the crowd."

She invited Ocasio-Cortez to her group's Iftar dinner, and a few months later emailed the campaign to say her family still lived in the district and was interested in volunteering for AOC's campaign. She got a reply from the volunteer organizer Bilal Tahir, who promptly named Akhter a precinct captain. A few weeks later the dozen or so people who made up the early part of the campaign met at Akhter's parents apartment to drink Bengali chai tea. They laid a big map of the district on the floor and figured out how they would get the vote out of each neighborhood. Akhter told the group at that first meeting, "Someday someone is going to write a book about this campaign."

Part of their plan was to find field captains who actually lived (or at least had a connection to) the neighborhoods where they went hunting for votes, and another part of their plan was to go everywhere, regardless of how many votes they thought it would garner them. City Island is a conservative part of New York City, only accessible by a single three-lane bridge, a neighborhood of tiny homes and deep-fried fish shacks overlooking Long Island Sound. Late in the campaign, Michael Carter, who helped with fundraising and the field operation, realized they had nobody from City Island on their list of likely supporters.

So a bunch of them loaded into a van one Saturday, and knocked on every Democratic door.

They won City Island by seven votes.

"What I learned and what I think too few political folks understand is that your worst ratio in any precinct is typically 20/80. So the only reason you shouldn't go somewhere is if you are in legitimate fear of being physically harmed. But otherwise? If you're in an area that's 20/80 and you bump it up to 25, those votes count just the same," said Carter.

Carter got into left politics through reading Marx as part of his Contemporary Civilization course at Columbia, part of the university's required core curriculum. He worked for Sanders in 2016 and then got involved in New York City politics before getting involved in Ocasio-Cortez's race.

Which is to say there was no one type of person who was drawn to Ocasio-Cortez's campaign; they were mostly young, but they were of all races, ethnic backgrounds, education levels, and social classes and had varying levels of experience in political organizing. What they shared was a shock and outrage that someone as ill fit for the job as Donald Trump could become president. Fueled by rage and determination, many, for the first time in their lives, got involved in politics to combat him.

Daniel Bonthius had come to New York from Boston to be an actor. He had settled in Sunnyside, Queens, a one-time Irish American enclave that had become a haven over the last decade for people priced out of Brooklyn, and had been making ends meet as an actor and event planner. The day after the 2016 election, he woke up feeling the need to talk with like-minded people about what had just happened. He gathered a few neighbors together, and they met in a someone's living room, and eventually became the local chapter of Indivisible.

Indivisible was the brainchild of Ezra Levin and his wife, Leah Greenberg, both in their early thirties and both former congressional staffers on Capitol Hill. After grieving over the election of Trump with friends, the couple went home to Levin's parents' house in Texas for Thanksgiving and met up with an old college friend who was managing a Facebook group called Dumbledore's Army, a reference to the kindly professor in the Harry Potter books. In a matter of days the Facebook group had three thousand people who were committed to resisting Trump but weren't sure how. Protests in the street and writing letters to Paul Ryan seemed futile.

"We had this model in our minds, which was the Tea Party," Greenberg told an interviewer. "We knew that there were actually very effective ways to organize locally, to deploy that activism, to change the way that Congress thought, because we'd seen it used against us. And so we kind of looked at each other and we were like, 'Maybe we should just write a guide to replicating the Tea Party.'"[4]

While the rest of the family chomped on turkey and leftovers, Levin and Greenberg decamped to their laptops and started writing a guide for those interested in creating their own Tea Party of the Left.

"Trying to figure out how to resist the coming racist, plutocratic Trump/congressional onslaught? Calls and petitions aren't enough," Levin tweeted to his mere 650 followers. "To help, former congressional staff drafted this guide, drawing lessons from how the Tea Party stopped Obama."[5]

The document acknowledged that the Tea Party was racist and cruel in its motivations but that it was also remarkably effective because activists put pressure on their own members of Congress, and because activists in the various chapters, no matter how large or small, worked in close coordination with each other and with other groups to keep up the pressure. And the Tea Party was reactive and defensive; they didn't come up with their own alternatives, but were instead focused on shooting down the options offered by the White House and Congress.

"While the Tea Party activists were united by a core set of shared beliefs, they actively avoided developing their own policy agenda. Instead, they had an extraordinary clarity of purpose, united in opposition to President Obama. They didn't accept concessions and treated weak Republicans as traitors," the guide said.

They called on members of the liberal resistance to show up at their local representative's town hall meetings and demand answers, show up at their office and demand a meeting, and flood phone lines with calls about upcoming key votes. At the time, the GOP controlled the White House, the Senate, the House of Representatives, and, for all intents and purposes, the courts, leaving activists with seemingly little recourse.

The Indivisible guide offered this advice:

Stall the Trump agenda by forcing them to redirect energy away from their priorities. Congressional offices have limited time and limited people. A day that they spend worrying about you is a day that they're not ending Medicare, privatizing public schools, or preparing a Muslim registry.

Sap Representatives' will to support or drive reactionary change. If you do this right, you will have an outsized impact.

Every time your MoC [member of Congress] signs on to a bill, takes a position, or makes a statement, a little part of his or her mind will be thinking: "How am I going to explain this to the angry constituents who keep showing up at my events and demanding answers?"

Reaffirm the illegitimacy of the Trump agenda. The hard truth is that Trump, McConnell, and Ryan will have the votes to cause some damage. But by objecting as loudly and powerfully as possible, and by centering the voices of those who are most affected by their agenda, you can ensure that people understand exactly how bad these laws are from the very start—priming the ground for the 2018 midterms and their repeal when Democrats retake power.

Indivisible organizers encouraged those interested to form their own groups. Groups should be kept local, the document said, and small, at least at first. The document instructed activists on how to run and manage organizations and how to focus them on the work ahead.

"Keep people focused on the ultimate core strategy: applying pressure to your MoC to stop Trump," the document said, and organizers suggested rallying around a couple of core principles: (1) "Donald Trump's agenda will take America backwards and must be stopped," and (2) "In order to work together to achieve this goal, we must model the values of inclusion, tolerance, and fairness."

Within days the document had racked up hundreds of thousands of views, with everyone from former Clinton administration labor secretary Robert Reich to *Star Trek* star George Takei tweeting out promotion and praise. Indivisible groups formed all over the country, hundreds of them, in every congressional district, and they proceeded to make life difficult for Republicans in Congress.

Back in Queens, Bonthius and his neighbors decided to call themselves an Indivisible group, mostly in the hopes that affiliating with a national organization would increase their visibility. They canvassed for local progressive candidates, rallied against the IDC, and went to town halls. At one town hall, hosted by Congressman Joe Crowley, Jake DeGroot, a member of the local Indivisible group, confronted Crowley over taking corporate PAC money, and the two got into a heated exchange. Afterward another town hall attendee approached DeGroot and asked if he had heard about this woman running against Crowley, Alexandria Ocasio-Cortez. He reached out over Twitter—she just had a couple of hundred followers at the time—and invited her to the next meeting of the group.

It was Ocasio-Cortez's first constituent house party, and the group was impressed. "It just seemed like she is a real person running for office," said Bonthius, who became one of her closest campaign and then congressional aides. "Everybody in the room, we are all the same generation, the same generation she is, and there is just this comfort level, like, you are one of us. You are going to be fighting for us."[6]

DeGroot, a theater lighting designer by trade, had been at Zuccotti Park for Occupy Wall Street, but he had lost the political bug until Trump's election in November 2016. He ended up going to work for Ocasio-Cortez's campaign and even designed a canvassing app, called Reach, which upturned the traditional way campaigns reach their targeted voters. Typically, campaigns have canvassing lists of people who are registered to vote and who have voted in the last couple of elections. The campaigns may know something about the voters from their neighborhood or other demographic data, and they send canvassers out to record whether or not those voters are likely to vote for them. Reach, though, was focused on bringing new voters into the process, and so it allowed Ocasio-Cortez's campaign team to record interactions with any voters anywhere, bringing them into the political process with just a few taps of their phone.

Another person invited to the Queens Stand Up rally in Forest Hills was Hawk Newsome, an attorney and civil rights activist. Newsome had been involved in politics and protest his whole life— his parents met at a civil rights rally in 1969—and he had gone on

to work in the Bronx district attorney's office and in local organizations before starting Black Lives Matter of Greater New York.
Black Lives Matter began after George Zimmerman, a white man
who was volunteering with his neighborhood watch in his Sanford,
Florida, housing complex, confronted and shot Trayvon Martin, an
unarmed African American teenager. Zimmerman was later acquit-
ted of murder, which led Alicia Garza, a domestic workers' rights
organizer, to post on Facebook what she called "a love note to black
people": "Black people. I love you. I love us. Our lives matter, Black
Lives Matter," she wrote, urging Black people to get active in their
communities. Patrisse Cullors, a human rights activist with the Ella
Baker Center for Human Rights, in Oakland, California, and who
first met Garza a decade before on the dance floor in Providence,
Rhode Island, where both were attending an organizers' conference,
responded with the hashtag #BlackLivesMatter. The two, along
with writer and activist Opal Tometi, worked to turn the hashtag
into a movement.[7]

Black Lives Matter was, in its conception, as much a protest
against police brutality and a racially oppressive government as it
was against a model of Black politics that had held in place for over
half a century. That model was deeply tied to a top-down power
structure and to the Black church and, importantly, to the Democratic Party. Black Lives Matter, on the other hand, was diffuse,
with organizations and actions happening around the country with
only sometimes the slimmest connection to one another, and it was
largely leaderless as well, even though various figures, including the
founders, emerged as spokespeople.

The movement grew exponentially in the second Obama term, as
there were more incidents of unarmed African American men killed
by the police, incidents that were often captured on video and sent
out to the world and, in some cases, streamed live as they occurred.
Black Lives Matter activists from around the country gathered in
Ferguson, Missouri, after the white police officer who had killed Michael Brown, an African American teenager, was not indicted by a
grand jury. One of the leaders of "Freedom Ride to Ferguson," a call

for activists to travel to Ferguson in honor of Brown, was Aislinn Pulley, an activist against police violence in Chicago and one of the founders of the local Black Lives Matter chapter there.

The Black Lives Matter movement was grassroots, and it mostly eschewed politics, with Pulley representing that strain of engagement. In the last year of his presidency, Obama invited civil rights leaders from an older generation, like the Reverend Al Sharpton and the late congressman John Lewis who, as chairman of the Student Nonviolent Coordinating Committee, helped organize the March on Washington in 1963. Obama also invited leaders of Black Lives Matter, but Pulley declined to attend.

"As a radical, Black organizer, living and working in a city that is now widely recognized as a symbol of corruption and police violence, I do not feel that a handshake with the president is the best way for me to honor Black History Month or the Black freedom fighters whose labor laid the groundwork for the historic moment we are living in," Pulley wrote in an op-ed explaining her decision to not participate. She went on:

> I was under the impression that a meeting was being organized to facilitate a genuine exchange on the matters facing millions of Black and Brown people in the United States. Instead, what was arranged was basically a photo opportunity and a 90-second sound bite for the president. I could not, with any integrity, participate in such a sham that would only serve to legitimize the false narrative that the government is working to end police brutality and the institutional racism that fuels it. For the increasing number of families fighting for justice and dignity for their kin slain by police, I refuse to give its perpetrators and enablers political cover by making an appearance among them.
>
> If the administration is serious about addressing the issues of Black Lives Matter Chicago . . . they can start by meeting the simple demands of families who want transparency, and who want police that kill Black people unjustly to be fired, indicted and held accountable.[8]

Hawk Newsome was as apolitical as an activist gets. In 2016, he protested both the Democratic and Republican conventions with a sign that said "I ain't voting until Black lives matter," hoping that by holding out he and thousands like him could get the Democratic Party to prioritize criminal justice issues and to make a serious play for the African American vote instead of assuming it was theirs.

Newsome's strategy didn't work. By the next year, Black Lives Matter started to wane as a movement as Trump grabbed the media spotlight, but Black Lives Matter of Greater New York remained active, and in 2017, Ocasio-Cortez reached out to seek their endorsement.

At the time, Ocasio-Cortez had no local endorsements. The entire political establishment, even from the most left-leaning quarters like the Working Families Party and Make the Road New York, an immigrants rights organization, endorsed Crowley, moves they would quickly come to regret.

Ocasio-Cortez met with Newsome and some other members of his group in Lincoln Square and laid out the case for her candidacy. His group endorsed her on the spot, the only candidate for federal office they did endorse. If Black Lives Matter of New York had felt ignored by the political process so far, here at last was a candidate speaking their language.

"We believe in endorsing revolutionaries," Newsome said. "And here was this young, Latinx woman running for office with a revolutionary spirit."

The Black Lives Matter group loved that Ocasio-Cortez had gone to Standing Rock, and they loved that she had arrived at their meeting alone, without an entourage of aides. She ended up marching alongside them as the group took to the streets in 2018 to protest police violence.

"She sold us on her vision of what politics should be. She had ideas about the redistribution of wealth, she cared about immigration police and police brutality. It was a vision that aligned with our vision," Newsome said.

As winter turned to spring and spring to early summer, Ocasio-Cortez's campaign began to gain steam. Those young voters in the district who thrilled to the message that Sanders delivered two years before found in Ocasio-Cortez a worthy heir.

A turning point came when the Ocasio-Cortez campaign introduced its only ad of the campaign. Called "The Courage to Change," the two-minute spot shows Ocasio-Cortez getting ready in the morning in her Bronx apartment, fixing her hair, putting on makeup, taking the subway, ordering coffee from her local bodega, and talking to voters. As Crowley had moved up in the ranks in Washington, he settled with his family in the suburbs of northern Virginia, something that Ocasio-Cortez attacked him for, beginning with that ad.

"Women like me aren't supposed to run for office," Ocasio-Cortez intones over swelling music. "I am an educator, an organizer, a working-class New Yorker. I have worked with expectant mothers, I have waited tables, and I have led classrooms, and going into politics wasn't in the plan."

The ad then flips to a picture of Crowley speaking, as it happened, on Fox News, cut with images of luxury towers that were being built just outside the district Ocasio-Cortez was trying to represent.

"But after twenty years of the same representation, we have to ask: Who has New York been changing for?" she asks in the ad. "Every day it gets harder for working families like mine to get by. The rent gets higher, healthcare covers less, and our income stays the same. It is clear that these changes haven't been for us, and we deserve a champion," she says, as the spot intersperses shots of Ocasio-Cortez giving a rousing speech at a meeting of the Democratic Socialists of America with shots of the district and her walking around it.

The script was written by Ocasio-Cortez herself, but the rest of the video was the work of two Detroit-based democratic socialists,

Naomi Burton and Nick Hayes. They reached out to Ocasio-Cortez on Twitter after they heard about her campaign on Facebook and offered to do the campaign video. The whole ad cost less than ten thousand dollars, mostly because it was shot using volunteers and family members of the candidate, in her apartment and on the campaign trail.

Both Burton and Hayes had worked in advertising and corporate communications but had grown disillusioned with the work. Hayes recalled two instances regarding Detroit's *Metro Times* newspaper that turned him off: one, when a Los Angeles director parachuted into Detroit for the day, interviewing locals and getting shots of the city to make a major beer brand seem cool and authentic, and another when he was shooting a commercial inside a Lansing, Michigan, factory and was overwhelmed by the stench of plastic chemicals.

"I remember thinking that I only had to be there for a few hours, but the workers had to come every day and work in those conditions," he told the paper. "I thought, 'Why am I spending any time trying to help them sell more styrofoam?'"[9]

The entire campaign was a homespun affair, but it was Ocasio-Cortez who was in charge of the messaging. In *Knock Down the House*, the Netflix documentary that is partially about her run, Ocasio-Cortez piece-by-piece deconstructs a Crowley mailer.

"Look at this thing. Everybody in the district got this Victoria's Secret catalogue of my opponent," said Ocasio-Cortez, holding up a generic-looking Crowley mailer. She contrasted it with her eye-popping purple palm card. "This is the difference between an organizer and a strategist. What am I trying to do? Two things. I want them to know my name and I want them to know that they need to vote. OK, vote for her. Why?" she said, flipping the card over and pointing at the bullet points on the back side: "End the War on Drugs. 100% renewable energy. Tuition free public college."

Then she reads from Crowley's mailer: "'Taking on Donald Trump in Washington. Delivering for Queens and the Bronx.' 'Deliver' is insider talk. Deliver means pork. Oh, Alex, you are being way too harsh, let's give him a chance. OK, let's give him a chance, let's open it up. We got this big, beautiful spread here," she said, showing pictures of a smiling Crowley greeting children and neighborhood residents. "Where is the primary date? Democrat Joe Crowley is leading the fight against Donald Trump. There is nothing about the path forward here. Trump, three times. Commitments, zero times."

Ocasio-Cortez's mailer was made by Tandem Design, a company helmed by people who knew Ocasio-Cortez from her bartending days. The yellow, blue, and purple mailers were different from the typical red, white, and blue ones that most campaigns use, and they featured Ocasio-Cortez's striking visage boldly looking off into the distance at some uncertain future, her eyes upturned as if what was to come was hopeful instead of threatening. Tandem Design borrowed from revolutionary posters of the farm workers movement of the 1960s and used an upside-down exclamation point to highlight Ocasio-Cortez's heritage in a district of mostly minorities.

"Politicians are tough egotistical beasts when it comes to branding. I've seen amazing identities chewed down by calls to add more stripes and stars and flags," the founder of Tandem, Scott Starrett, told *Vox*. "Being a homogenous or safe candidate, visually, really communicates something to the public. It makes sense for conservatives to have conservative identities. Why do progressives have identities exactly the same as their colleagues across the aisle? It fits into a coding system of, 'Don't look here. You know the drill.'"[10]

"They had spent two years talking politics at their local watering hole with her," campaign manager Ramos Rios said. "And then she met with them for a couple of hours and told them what she was looking for, but they had this full history going back years with her. The rest of the campaign thought the yellow was too much, but she was insistent. It was supposed to look like a comic book in a way— Medicare for All, Get Money Out of Politics—it's superhero stuff."

There were two debates, one televised on the local news station NY1, and one at a local Jewish community center. In the first, Ocasio-Cortez came in visibly nervous, according to people who were backstage with her. She arrived with two other people, a friend of hers and her boyfriend, and they stood in a circle and did breathing exercises and gave each other pep-talk "affirmations." "It was totally human, but it was some real hippy shit," said a person backstage with them.

At the debate table, Ocasio-Cortez looked coiled to pounce on Crowley. She had practiced relentlessly before, and planned to hit Crowley on a House ethics investigation from years before on his fundraising practices with the line, "Mr. Crowley, do you have an ethics problem?" but in the end was unable to get the line out. Afterward, she told me she wished she had been able to hit him harder. As it was, she slammed Crowley for raising his family in the DC suburbs. "If a person loves their community," she said during the debate, "they would choose to raise their family here, they would choose to send their kids to our schools, and they would breathe our air and drink our water. It takes away a fundamental interest and understanding of our communities when we raise our families somewhere else."

Crowley tried to counter Ocasio-Cortez by accusing her of being soft on gun control. The Crowley campaign had dug up a comment that Ocasio-Cortez had made earlier on a Reddit "Ask Me Anything" online forum in which Ocasio-Cortez had, in response to a question about not becoming "siloed" in her own political universe: "Locally I happen to support NYC's more strict take on gun control. But I also believe that there needs to be flexibility on the national level. NYC isn't New Mexico."[11] After Crowley brought it up at the NY1 debate, AOC responded by accused Crowley of searching for dirt on her by "trolling Internet forums." He pledged to support Ocasio-Cortez if she won and asked if she would make the same pledge to him, a smart move since, by that point, she clearly had a following but also seemed destined to lose. Ocasio-Cortez deflected. "I represent not a campaign but a movement," she said, noting she would have to go back to her endorsers, groups like DSA and Black Lives Matter, before she could make any decision on that score.

And Ocasio-Cortez hit him for not calling for the abolition of ICE, a call that had grown in power in the weeks and months before the election. "If this organization is fascist," she said, slamming the tabletop with her hands, "then why don't you adopt the stance to eliminate it? This is a moral problem, and your response is to apply more paperwork to this question."

By the race's final weekend, people had come from all over the country to volunteer, sleeping on couches or in their cars. There were forty people lined up outside of her office to knock on doors. A sound truck, featuring a billboard-sized AOC poster, was crawling neighborhoods in the Queens and Bronx. Internal Crowley polls still had him up by 30 points, and no one really gave AOC a chance, but it was clear she had caught on.

And then, Ocasio-Cortez did something unheard of in politics: she skipped town.

While the Crowley forces were holding a big rally on a rainy Saturday, Ocasio-Cortez was thousands of miles away at the US-Mexico border to protest the Trump administration's child separation policy.

It led to striking visuals that rocketed around social media of Ocasio-Cortez pleading with guards at the gate, but it seemed suicidal politically. It was Ocasio-Cortez's idea, and no one tried to talk her out of it.

"As a campaign manager, yes, it is hard not to have the candidate present for the final weekend," said Ramos Rios. "But here's the thing: You are talking about a district that is 50 percent immigrants. And so you're talking about a candidate who is recognizing what's important to them and is highlighting it.

"We could see a path to victory at that point, but she also had a spotlight and if she could take that spotlight and highlight something that mattered to the people in her district, that's what she was going to do. It wasn't about winning. It was a movement. Victory comes in getting people to see somebody who's willing to represent her district wholly, even if that means for her personally, it might not be a gain. She might go back to being a bartender and a waitress. She was going to take that little bit of spotlight and highlight an issue, and that was incredibly important to people in her district."

On Election Day, the streets of the district were flooded with volunteers from both sides, but it was clear that many of the those there for Crowley were connected in some way to the Queens political machine; they were staffers for local elected officials or members of a local political club. Shawna Morlock, the hairdresser from Astoria, stood outside of a polling place in her neighborhood to urge voters to pull the lever for AOC, but she thought something was up when she got to talking with a person, a firefighter, who was there on behalf of Crowley's campaign. He was a union guy, and as they started talking, she was surprised to hear him say good things about Donald Trump and bad things about immigrants. Later, he admitted he wasn't a Democrat at all but was there at the polling place because his union asked him to be.

Ocasio-Cortez spent much of Election Day tweeting photos of places where she thought the Crowley forces had hung illegal signs, and then accusing the Crowley forces of taking down her signs and putting theirs up illegally. There was no evidence of it, and it wasn't the only baseless accusation thrown out by Ocasio-Cortez during the campaign. She accused the incumbent of not having bilingual campaign literature, which was false, and of Crowley acolytes tampering with election machines, which would have been a violation of state law and for which there was also no evidence. Crowley couldn't make one of the debates because he had a previous commitment in another part of the district, so he sent a surrogate in his place, a local city councilwoman named Annabel Palma, and Ocasio-Cortez accused him of deliberately attempting to confuse voters by sending a Latina in his stead.

Ocasio-Cortez's mother, Bianca, joined the campaign for the final days. She became a regular campaign volunteer, joining the others who had been inspired by Ocasio-Cortez's campaign, and allowing herself to feel the faint hope that her daughter could actually win. As they were waiting for the election results, Morlock told Bianca to just relax, saying, "She is going to be president one day, just you watch," to which Bianca replied, "Don't jinx it!"

As the team members finished their day on the streets, Ocasio-Cortez gathered with a few of them in a pocket park in the Bronx. At polling stations across the district, the enthusiasm for her seemed palpable, yet, still, no one believed she could win. Surely, they figured, there was a reserve army of Crowley supporters who could pull this off.

"No matter what happens, this does not stop here," Ocasio-Cortez said to her supporters as evening fell. "I want every single one of you, to stay active, to keep pushing. Once people have been woken up, they don't go back to sleep."

The minute the polls closed, the Crowley forces knew the race was over. There had been massive turnout in areas good for Ocasio-Cortez and very limited turnout in Crowley's precincts. The Crowley election night party was a new bistro on Northern Boulevard in Jackson Heights. The room didn't have any TVs, and so the people in attendance, who were most of the city's political class, including at least three people then planning on running for mayor in three years and hoping to pay homage to one of the most powerful people in the city, had no idea what the early returns showed: that Ocasio-Cortez had opened up a big lead on Crowley. As more votes came in, the lead only widened. Crowley staffers were in tears. Local elected officials stormed off in disgust, with one suggesting that was why primaries were a bad idea. Some, seeing which way the wind was blowing, dashed out and headed up to Ocasio-Cortez's election night party in the Bronx. Crowley came in eventually to cheers. An amateur musician, Crowley's band was set up in a corner of the restaurant and, with the congressman on guitar and vocals, launched into a rip-roaring rendition of "Born to Run," dedicated to AOC.

"I may not have gotten proper credit for all the things I have done," Crowley said afterward while sipping on a beer as the band played "Ramblin' Man" behind him. "The people in this district know me. It was a Democratic primary at a time of low turnout. It is what it is."

"People know me as a national figure, not a local one," he added. "I think I always maintained my connectivity to the district. But at the end of the day it's not about me. It's about the people. I give my opponent, Alexandria Ocasio-Cortez, a lot of credit. She ran a good race."

Meanwhile, up in the Bronx, Ocasio-Cortez was in a car with her partner, Riley Roberts, and a few campaign staff were on their way to her election night party at a pool hall in the Bronx.

Naureen Akhter had made two cakes for the occasion, figuring that win or lose, the occasion called for cake. Ocasio-Cortez refused to look at the returns coming in, and so was genuinely shocked when a reporter for NY1 pulled her aside as she was declared the victor. Actor and activist Cynthia Nixon showed up to celebrate. Most media had been banned since they had not bothered to cover the race in the first place.

"I told you!" Morlock said when she saw Bianca Ocasio-Cortez standing off to the side, weeping tears of joy. "She is going to be president. I am calling it right now!"

Roberts was interviewed by People for Bernie, which live-streamed his words to the group's Facebook account, and he said they always had talked about something like this happening but never thought it would happen so soon. The crowd began to chant, "AOC! AOC!"

Ocasio-Cortez stood up on the bar and addressed her exhausted supporters: "This room won this seat! Every person out here changed America tonight. What is very clear is that this is not the end, this is the beginning. The message we sent to the world tonight is that it is not okay to put donors before your community. The message that we sent tonight is that sometime between midnight and darkness there is still hope for this nation. You have given this country hope that when you knock on your neighbor's door, when you come to them with love, when you come to them and tell them that no matter their stance, you are there for them, we can make change. What you have shown is that this nation is never beyond remedy, it is never beyond hope.

"Every person in this room is going to DC with me," she added. "We have to dedicate ourselves to this fight because I can't do it alone."

CHAPTER 3

HER REVOLUTION

To have called Bernie Sanders an underdog when he announced he was running for president in 2015 would have been a vast understatement. Prior to jumping in, he had been teasing a race for months, making stump speeches in the early primary states, rallying with workers and activists in Wisconsin and suburban California, places usually overlooked in presidential primaries, and distributing campaign cash through his political action committee to vulnerable red-state Democrats. And yet scarcely anyone had paid attention.

"I don't think there is a chance he will win," one of his supporters, an eighty-two-year-old woman, told me at an early rally for Sanders in New Hampshire in the summer of 2014, one where the Vermont senator refined his stump speech, railing against the billionaire class, the Koch Brothers, the fossil fuel lobby, and giant corporations.

"He's a socialist!" she exclaimed, thrusting her hands up in the air as if trying to force me to understand what she meant. "We aren't there yet. We may never get there."

In what was supposed to be a two-person race between Sanders and Hillary Clinton—and with the possibility that newly elected senator and liberal favorite Elizabeth Warren would accede to her supporters' wishes and jump in the race—most political commentators put Sanders's ceiling at around 15 percent of the electorate.

And even a figure that high was thought to be a result of a race in which there were only two choices. Far left candidates had, after all, often failed to make much of an impact, whether it was Dennis Kucinich in 2008, Howard Dean in 2004, or, in the general election, Ralph Nader in 2000, who, despite much hand-wringing, ended the race with under 3 percent of the vote.

But in a nation ground down after decades of widening inequality, stagnating wages, growing healthcare costs, ever higher levels of personal debt, and still not fully recovered from the economic collapse of 2008, Sanders caught on, despite the long odds against him.

It is an overused term in politics, but the Bernie Sanders campaign for president really did become a movement. Within a few weeks of announcing his candidacy, two hundred thousand people had signed up as volunteers.[1] By the time it was finished, Sanders had nearly 2.5 million donors, tens of thousands of people who had signed up to host his events, a Bernie for President subreddit with 188,000 subscribers—more than those for beer, cars, or porn.[2] He also gained an army of supportive techies, who created on average an app per week for the campaign, including one that organized volunteer phone banks, another called "Bernie BnB," which helped volunteers find places to stay on the trail, and a third that contained Sanders's policy positions and which the faithful could download and hand out to interested supporters while canvassing.

One of those who caught the Bernie bug was a waitress working in a Union Square restaurant named Alexandria Ocasio-Cortez. She didn't have much of a political bent before, save for her brief time interning in the office of Senator Ted Kennedy while in college at Boston University, but once Sanders mania swept the nation, the young Ocasio-Cortez was hooked. Coworkers and even customers recall her talking about the presidential race, and about Sanders specifically, to anyone who would listen in 2015 and 2016.

"I worked shoulder to shoulder with undocumented workers who often worked harder and hardest for the least amount of money. I was on my feet working twelve-hour days with no structured breaks. I didn't have healthcare. I wasn't being paid a living wage, and I didn't think that I deserved any of those things," Ocasio-Cortez told a rally of twenty-six thousand people in Queens when she made a surprise endorsement of Sanders in his 2020 race. "Because that is the script that we tell working people here and all over this country, that your inherent worth and value as a human being is dependent on an income that another person decided to underpay us. . . . It wasn't until I heard of a man by the name of Bernie Sanders that I began to question and assert and recognize my inherent value as a human being that deserves healthcare, housing, education, and a living wage."

She went on to describe how at various points in her life, she came to appreciate how Sanders was fighting for her, how her mother relied on Planned Parenthood for prenatal care, which Sanders fought for, how she relied on Children's Health Insurance Program as a kid, and how Sanders fought for universal healthcare, student debt relief, and civil rights. "I'm proud to say that the only reason that I had any hope in launching a long-shot campaign for Congress is because Bernie Sanders proved that you can run a grassroots campaign and win in an America where we almost thought it was impossible."

It was reported in the press after her victory that AOC was a Sanders delegate to the 2016 Democratic National Convention. It wasn't true. "I was just a scrub," she told me when I interviewed her for a story for *New York* magazine. "I was just an organizer in the South Bronx, and we were cutting turf out of a former nail salon not too far from 138th and Grand Concourse."

But Ocasio-Cortez is actually downplaying her involvement. She was known around the campaign in the Bronx as a "super volunteer," someone who showed up in the winter of 2015–16 to gather signatures to ensure that Sanders would be on the ballot, since, according to New York law, candidates need to gather signatures in each congressional district, and Sanders was lacking in New York's Fourteenth. Organizers remember her as earnest and probing, wanting to know how the mechanics of a campaign worked, and cracking up when canvassers would tell of Bronx residents who would confuse the "Bernie" on their pins for Bernie Madoff, the disgraced financier.

Ocasio-Cortez led canvassing events at the train station near her house, and when it came time for everyone to say why they were there, she told her story: her father dying young, her dual life between Westchester and the Bronx, and her struggle to afford healthcare while working as a waitress. On the day before the primary, she snapped a photo of campaign workers in white Bernie shirts making phone calls out of the campaign's South Bronx headquarters. She posted the picture to Reddit on the Sanders for President page.

"As a native Bronxite I am so proud of the campaign's work here. We are flipping voters to Bernie in droves, but with so many people here it's tough to get a gauge on our actual impact. It's the day before the primary and people are STILL making up their minds," she wrote in her first post to Reddit on April 18, 2016. "Really thanks for the opportunity to be a part of this movement for a greater and more just America. Let's keep pushing, pushing, pushing to the convention!"

Even though New York was something of a home base for Hillary Clinton—she had moved to the tony New York City suburb of Chappaqua before launching her own political career and had won statewide election to the Senate twice—Sanders vowed to compete hard, opening up campaign offices throughout the state and hosting mega rallies in Brooklyn and Manhattan with tens of thousands of fans in attendance. He opened up a campaign office in the South Bronx and held his first New York City rally there on March 31, 2016, before 10,500 people in St. Mary's Park while another 8,000 spilled into a nearby overflow space at a public ballfield where they watched the rally on giant screens. After introductions by actor Rosario Dawson and film director Spike Lee, Sanders pledged to cease getting the country engaged in costly and bloody wars in places like Iraq and to reinvest in jobs and education in the South Bronx and other distressed communities. "The enthusiastic crowd was diverse

'08 just so I could vote in the primary. I saw this post and thought there was no way my registration could be affected," she wrote, referring to an earlier post about how some registrations had been changed. "Checked anyway . . . and my voter affiliation has been changed. I am no longer affiliated with any party and as of today am ineligible to vote in the primary. Total shock."[4]

Ocasio-Cortez continued, "I used to be on the fence about the Open vs. Closed primary issue, but that has completely changed today. We need open primaries everywhere to prevent this from happening again. I am so hurt that my right to vote in this primary has been taken from me. Contacting my NY County registrar today and will update with what they say. Also shared my story on social media."

Later—it is unclear exactly how much later—AOC added an update:

> Just called my Board of Elections. Here is what happened—Hurricane Sandy hit during the last presidential election and as an emergency measure, Gov. Cuomo opened polling stations all over the state, allowing anybody to vote at any location so long as you signed an affidavit. I was stuck in NYC and voted outside my precinct, and apparently when I signed that affidavit my party affiliation was waived. I had no idea I was losing my party status when I did that. Even though the registration deadline is tomorrow, the party change deadline was in October. Really upsetting. Had I known this was the case I would have fixed this ages ago.

The story got picked up by the media, with the liberal website *ThinkProgress* writing a piece that included Ocasio-Cortez's story, which got picked up by *The Young Turks* show on YouTube.[5] Ocasio-Cortez then tweeted at the show's host, Cenk Uygur, who would have so much to do with her later political success, "@cenkuygur Hi Cenk! I'm Alexandria, the voter you mentioned in your NY voting piece tonight. Lmk if you can talk," Ocasio-Cortez wrote.

If the Bernie campaign eventually flamed out, it provided, in many ways, the infrastructure that helped Ocasio-Cortez get elected two years later. Back when Sanders was still in the exploratory phase of his campaign, a group of liberal activists and Democratic donors were trying to recruit Elizabeth Warren into the race. Hillary Clinton hadn't yet declared her candidacy, but she was already a juggernaut thanks to Ready for Hillary, a super PAC that served as a campaign-in-waiting as Clinton enjoyed her post–State Department life, raising millions of dollars and hiring dozens of staffers in the meantime.

And so a group of progressives launched Ready for Warren as a response, which Winnie Wong, a longtime activist, termed a "narrative intervention." At the time, it appeared as if Clinton would waltz to the nomination. With no one running to her left, it meant there would be room for progressive ideas, which had been gaining more traction as a number of cities adopted a minimum wage that approached fifteen dollars an hour and Black Lives Matter protests took over the streets around the country. Even the threat of Warren meant there would be a space to the left of Clinton.

But Ready for Warren was meant more to lure the Massachusetts senator into the race. Even though she had only been elected two years prior, Warren was already a liberal favorite, someone who raised a staggering $42 million in her first race and whose YouTube clips went viral. Ready for Warren raised less than $200,000 and hired a couple of staffers in the early primary states, but Warren remained adamant that she was not interested in a campaign.

And so the group broke up, but two of its founders, Winnie Wong and Charles Lenchner, quickly pivoted to a new project: getting behind the progressive who was actually in the race.

Both were veterans of Occupy Wall Street, the 2011 protests that began with a plea on the website for *Adbusters*, an anti-capitalist magazine, calling for a Million Man March on Wall Street. At the time, the country was only three years removed from a financial crisis that shook the global economy and plunged America into its worst recession since the 1930s. In October 2009, the unemployment rate peaked at 10 percent, and a little over a year later the recovery had been slow and fitful. The Tea Party had begun in earnest in the spring of 2009 and by 2011 had stormed into power into Washington, threatening to slow the recovery even further by demanding government spending cuts just as more government spending was needed to juice the economy. The short piece in *Adbusters*, which was emailed to the magazine's digital subscribers, featured a woman twirling atop the Wall Street bull while tear gas and black-clad protesters massed in the distance. The image soon would get repurposed into Occupy Wall Street's logo, calling on Americans to gather in New York City's financial district, much as Egyptians were gathering in Tahrir Square to protest the autocratic regime there.

In part, the *Adbusters* piece said:

Could an uprising like this happen in America? Over 25 million folks are now unemployed, 2.8 million homes are in foreclosure while the investment bankers who brought this economic misery cynically reap obscene bonuses and rewards. Blatant corruption rules at the heart of American democracy. And with corporations now treated as people, big business money dictates who is elected to Congress and what laws they shall pass. America has devolved into a corporate state ruled by and for the megacorps. What would it take for the people of America to suddenly rise up and say "Enough!"? If we want to spark a popular uprising in the West—like a million man march on Wall Street—then let's get organized, let's strategize, let's think things through.

A few months later, *Adbusters* added another post, this one more specific: instead of the "alpha male" model of the anti-globalization protests of the late 1990s, what if the "90,000 redeemers, rebels and radicals out there" gathered "as one big swarm," leaderless and, frankly, directionless, except for how they directed themselves.

What if, the article asked, "we talk to each other in various phys-ical gatherings and virtual people's assemblies . . . we zero in on what our one demand will be, a demand that awakens the imagination and, if achieved, would propel us toward the radical democracy of the future . . . and then we go out and seize a square of singular sym-bolic significance and put our asses on the line to make it happen."[6]

The writers called for twenty thousand people to flood into Lower Manhattan—"the financial Gomorrah of America"—to "set up tents, kitchens, peaceful barricades and occupy Wall Street for a few months." And they called for the group to make one demand, repeated incessantly: "that Barack Obama ordain a Presidential Commission tasked with ending the influence money has over our representatives in Washington. It's time for DEMOCRACY NOT CORPORATOCRACY."

Adbusters saw corruption in the political realm as something that both the Left and the Right could agree on, and if the group of twenty-thousand strong held together week after week, their de-mands would become impossible for the political leadership of the country to ignore without making it clear that they cared more for corporations than people.

They set a date for September 17 and explicitly referenced the Tea Party as their model, but Occupy Wall Street would dismantle half of America's military and reinstate Glass-Steagall, a 1933 act that separated investment banks from retail banks and had been repealed under the Clinton administration, leading to the Great Recession, according to some economists, and finally, leading to the jailing of corporate criminals.

"Beginning from one simple demand—a presidential commis-sion to separate money from politics—we start setting the agenda for a new America," the editors wrote.

Readers and activists around the country took up the call in ways *Adbusters* could not have imagined. Protesters flocked to town squares in more than seventy American cities and hundreds more around the world; hundreds of thousands of people in the United States participated in one form or another, most notably in New

York, where hundreds camped out for weeks at Zuccotti Park in Lower Manhattan.

But the protesters didn't follow the original exhortation—"let's get organized, let's strategize, let's think things through"—and even though the protests introduced to the wider public the concept of "the 99 percent," a statement of mass solidarity against an oligarchic 1 percent, they quickly became more concerned with fetishizing their own democratic processes, resisting police and government authority, and building their own self-sustaining community out of doors. They did not make real demands on power and certainly not on the political system. The movement began to wane as the weather turned colder, and then ended finally when Mayor Mike Bloomberg decided the group could no longer camp in Zuccotti Park and sent the police in to clear away the tents and camping gear.

Sanders was one of the first elected officials to praise the protests, telling CNN, "I applaud them. They are speaking to the real anger and frustration that millions of Americans feel at a time when the middle class is collapsing, poverty is increasing, the people on top are doing phenomenally and the people who caused this damn recession in the first place, the folks on Wall Street, because of their greed and illegal behavior, you know what their punishment has been? They're now making more money than they ever made before.

"So what the demonstrators are saying, there's something wrong with that picture and they're exactly correct."[7]

When Sanders ran, he took up many of the same issues that Occupy protesters had made central: inequality, the concentration of power and wealth in the hands of too few, and the corruption of the political system. And some of the original Occupy protesters, like Lenchner and Wong, who were looking to make the movement more permanent, decided to get involved with the Sanders campaign. "Occupy was a reaction to the financial collapse, to what happened because of Wall Street's power to destroy the economy, and Bernie's campaign is the one that has been consistently focused on the role of the '1 Percent,' large corporations and financial institutions," Lenchner told an interviewer. "It's a very natural connection."[8]

But it was also a chance to move protest and social activism into a new realm, a realm that, frankly, had not been tried much before. Since the civil rights era, activism had a tendency to curdle into its own self-reinforced sphere. The point was to rally your own side to the cause, to attract media attention with public spectacle, and to increase visibility to increase membership and donations. Legislation wasn't proposed or fought over, but if it was, it was done by paid lobbyists in Washington, DC. Protesters didn't run for office. They protested. Movements were afraid of leaders and afraid of top-down power structures, and seemingly most afraid of seizing power for themselves.

"There's a tension in activist and protest movements, and the tension is [that] a lot of people who have really bitter feelings towards electoral politics or the Democratic Party or really any institution that has existed for a while and has money and power," said Lenchner. "There are a lot of people that are going to be anti–all that because they're younger, they're new or they've been on the short end of the stick too many times to have faith in it. But there are also a lot of other people that are kind of like me, and they understand that there are a spectrum of possibilities inside and outside the system, which is why you can knock doors on Monday and take to the streets on a Tuesday."

Which is what People for Bernie was—a protest movement that became a political one.

The Occupy movement "didn't lead to electoral victories, and I wanted to change that," Wong told an interviewer.[9]

And so Wong and Lenchner gathered dozens of their fellow Occupy vets and other activists and posted an open letter on the newly created People for Bernie website:

We are activists and organizers trying to build a broad, effective movement for democratic change. We come from different backgrounds, and were inspired by different issues and fights for peace, rights and the planet. Our goal is a government that carries out the will of the people, and not serve to increase the profits of the 1% at the expense of the rest of us.

To that end we support Bernie Sanders in his bid to become the presidential nominee of the Democratic Party. We stand firmly behind Senator Sanders as the strongest progressive possibility in the race right now. His commitment to our values is one of long standing commitment. Sanders is the bold alternative.

As a truly progressive candidate for the Democratic Party nomination, Senator Sanders has the chance to inspire millions of Americans with policy proposals that put the interests of the 99%, front and center.

Franklin D. Roosevelt called out the "economic royalists" of his day. Senator Sanders is picking up the banner. He answers to "We the People" and not to the corporate and financial sectors. Bernie brings the kind of leadership that is necessary to building a real, living democracy.

The initiators of this letter are veteran grassroots organizers of Occupy Wall Street, and are joined by many energized brothers and sisters we have met along the way. In September 2011, our efforts changed the narrative of American politics, helping to focus it on the issues of our time: inequality, surrender to the power of concentrated wealth, the corruption of our democracy by moneyed interests, and the need for solutions as radical as our problems.

We are signing as individuals hoping to kickstart a small "d" democratic movement. People for Bernie won't be a corporate-style, staff-driven, controlled-message, top-down enterprise. It will reflect diverse constituencies from a broad range of movements, which in many cases haven't seen the Democratic Party as a home for their deepest aspirations. It will reflect our commitment to fundamental change, not just a change of faces at the top of the political pyramid. People for Bernie will reflect the urgency of more and fiercer grassroots political activity at the base.

We call on all other progressive forces to unite behind Sanders so we can have a united front in this important campaign.[10]

The goal was unprecedented on a presidential campaign, merging activism with grassroots politics and led by someone with feet in both camps. "We cared a great deal about a kind of politics that didn't differentiate between the official Democratic institutions and 'street heat'—people willing to put their bodies on the line," Wong told me.

People for Bernie was funded mostly by the National Nurses Union, a key early Sanders backer but with no official connection or coordination with the campaign. Still, the union provided a place for people to get involved without getting linked up to the actual campaign, and to do so in a way that gave them creative freedom. Whether you wanted to make memes on the Internet or rent a bus and tour around the country talking to people about Sanders, People for Bernie would help facilitate that. They were often the first people on the ground in most states where Sanders competed; Sanders caught fire too late for the campaign to have done any long-term planning. Lenchner was a veteran of Dennis Kucinich's 2004 and 2008 campaigns, and had seen that left-wing campaigns fail by not giving space to the people inspired by the movement. And they were determined the Sanders campaign would not make the same mistake.

"This is a story about a revolution, and the story is being co-created by everybody," said Wong in 2016.

The campaign created hundreds of miniature groups for people to get involved in—African Americans for Bernie, Pet Lovers for Bernie, Gay Veterans for Bernie, and more—and while the campaign's organizing model found people who could host phone-banking parties and knock on doors, People for Bernie tried to find activists and civic leaders grounded in local communities, encouraging them to reach out to their networks on behalf of the campaign.

When the campaign came to New York, People for Bernie set up a phone bank in Zuccotti Park, and, in a further nod to their Occupy roots, produced half a million broadsheet newspapers that featured art, essays, and a call to vote for Bernie Sanders. The group spawned millions of DIY Sanders-inspired paraphernalia, including free online clip art for use as stickers or on sweatshirts, and helped mobilize over a hundred thousand people to host house parties or grassroots events at their homes. But their biggest contribution may have been the #FeelTheBern hashtag, which became more popular during the 2016 campaign than #Hillary2016.

"We knew from the experience of Occupy that as soon as Bernie would enter the race, thousands of people would immediately say, 'I'm a leader. What am I going to do now?'" Lenchner told me. "And if you do nothing to prepare the ground for it, then you have people going a thousand different directions at once. But if you do a little bit of prep work, if you get in front of it, you can sort of get people to willingly align themselves with each other. Sort of like a school of fish. Schools of fish don't have a leader, they just do it all together. But it takes a certain kind of effort."

The official Sanders campaign looked at the fervor their candidate inspired with a mix of bemusement and bewilderment, and never knew quite what to make of it. They resisted efforts on behalf of People for Bernie to become an arm of the campaign, or even to become vendors to the campaign, and wouldn't lend the group their blessing when they tried to coordinate. And so People for Bernie became something of a super PAC without any money, one whose resource was an army of enthusiastic volunteers instead of dollars.

"Bernie earned his popularity by being good on the issues," said Lenchner. "The problem was, how do you translate that popularity into very accessible mass action online and off. That's a slightly different issue than whether or not someone's popular. It's sort of like, George Takei is popular online, but if he tried to organize a thousand rallies he would probably fail at it. There's a missing connector. And that's the part that we played."

The People for Bernie Facebook page grew to have two million followers, making it the largest progressive community online. But eventually it became clear that Sanders was not going to be the nominee, and so the denizens of People for Bernie needed to plot their next move. In June 2016, more than three thousand of his loyal supporters gathered in Chicago for a two-day "People's

Summit." Their answer was, in part, to take the Sanders movement local, by running democratic socialists and other Sanders-inspired candidates down ballot for school board, city council, and state legislative seats.

But much as People for Bernie and the official Sanders campaign couldn't figure out a way to work together when Sanders was running for the Democratic nomination, so the Sanders post-campaign plan ended up swallowing its smaller grassroots counterpart.

Sanders had never planned on being president and never could have imagined that his candidacy would turn into a nationwide sensation. He would have been content to sit the entire campaign out if Elizabeth Warren had run. Soon after he announced his candidacy, Sanders met with Larry Cohen, a longtime friend and the head of the Communications Workers of America (CWA), a labor union of flight attendants, journalists, broadcast technicians, and electrical workers. Sitting in Sanders's dumpy campaign office in Washington, DC, Cohen asked Sanders if he really thought he was going to be the next president of the United States. This was soon after Sanders announced, back when the prospect of him seriously challenging Hillary Clinton and the entire Democratic Party establishment seemed ludicrous. Sanders put his hand on Cohen's shoulder and said, "Larry, I am not doing this to be president of the United States."

The point of Sanders's run, in other words, was to pull the party to the left and give Democrats uncomfortable with the prospect of a Clinton coronation a place to rally around.

But within twelve months, Sanders and his supporters were in a different place. After going toe-to-toe with Clinton across the country, it was time to figure out what the future would look like. Sanders saw November 2016 in much the same way everyone else did: a certain Clinton victory. His supporters had self-organized all over the country into small, autonomous outfits, from the SF Berniecrats in San Francisco to the Citizens for an Engaged Electorate in Williston, Florida, and Studizens for Safe Streets in Everett, Washington, to across New York State, where a number of groups like Bronx Progressives and Tioga County Progressive Committee had organized into an umbrella group called New York Progressive Action Network. What to do with all of this liberal energy?

The answer was Our Revolution, which would carry the Sanders movement forward during the coming Clinton presidency.

"Election days come and go, but the struggle for economic, social, racial and environmental justice continues," Sanders wrote in an email to supporters eleven days after the Democratic National Convention, where Clinton was formally handed the nomination. His email outlined "the next steps for our political revolution."

"Our goal will be the same as in our campaign: We must work to transform American society by making our political and economic systems work for all of us, not just the 1 percent," Sanders wrote. "Together, we can revitalize our democracy, empower new progressive leaders and educate the public about the critical issues facing our country."

The goal of the group at the outset was threefold: to bring millions of new people, mostly the young and working class, into the political system, to support progressive candidates "from the school board to the US Senate," and finally to do "what the corporate media does not do: Elevating political consciousness by educating the public about the most pressing issues confronting our nation and the bold solutions needed to address them."

Two weeks later, Sanders and his new group, Our Revolution, hosted a livestream that broadcast into some 2,600 house parties for 40,000 people, while hundreds of thousands more watched in the comfort of their own living rooms.

"I think the question on the minds of a whole lot of people is, 'Okay, we ran a great campaign. We woke up the American people. But where do we go from here?'" Sanders said. Referring to the group's platform, which was posted on its website and called for the election of one hundred Sanders-like candidates and victory in seven state-ballot initiatives around the country, Sanders declared,

"If anybody thinks that document, and what is in that platform, is going to be on a shelf collecting dust, they are sadly mistaken. We are going to make that document the blueprint for moving forward in this country. We changed the conversation regarding the possibilities of our country. That is what we changed."

Our Revolution, however, nearly blew up on launch. There was some grumbling from the start when the organization decided to operate as a 501(c)(4), a designation in the tax code reserved for social welfare organizations and expressly forbidden from political work. Such limitations have been mostly obliterated in a post–*Citizens United* world, but still it didn't make much sense for an organization for which part of its very existence was to endorse and support candidates for office. Plus, like other nonprofits (but not political organizations), 501(c)(4) organizations did not have to disclose their donors. The setup seemed out of step with a politician who had railed against dark money in politics and pushed for greater transparency in political giving.

Eyebrows were raised further when Sanders's wife, Jane, was named to the board, suggesting that the organization would be little more than a super PAC for Sanders's political interests. When Jeff Weaver, who had served as a senior adviser to the campaign, was named as the head of Our Revolution, mass defections followed. Weaver had been a longtime aide to Sanders and was as close a staffer to the senator as anyone in Washington could be, but his leadership of the 2016 campaign left bruised feelings among newer staffers, who felt that he had curbed some of their innovative ideas and had not given them credit for turning the Sanders message into a movement spread over social media and the Internet.

"It's about both the fundraising and the spending: Jeff would like to take big money from rich people including billionaires and spend it on ads," Claire Sandberg told *Politico* just before quitting her position as the organizing director of Our Revolution. "That's the opposite of what this campaign and this movement are supposed to be about and after being very firm and raising alarm the staff felt that we had no choice but to quit."

The organization pushed for Hillary Clinton to come out against the Dakota Access Pipeline and for Congress to kill the Trans Pacific Partnership, a major trade deal that Obama orchestrated over the objections of the party's Left. Our Revolution remained in turmoil throughout much of 2016, as Sanders returned to the Senate, campaigned for Clinton, and started working on his own book about the movement. Candidates who were favorites of the Left and endorsed by Sanders—like Tim Canova, a law professor who was running for a congressional seat held by Debbie Wasserman Schultz, a chair of the Democratic National Committee—saw what they viewed as bias against them and one that favored Hillary Clinton. Canova told *In These Times* that he'd been "left hanging" by Sanders after Our Revolution formed, when, thanks to its new tax status, it could no longer communicate directly with candidates.[11]

After Trump's win, however, the group found its purpose, even as it remained mired in infighting. Nina Turner, a charismatic state senator from Ohio, had lost a bid for Ohio secretary of state in 2014 before endorsing Hillary Clinton. However, she switched her endorsement to Sanders and eventually became president of Our Revolution, while LarryCohen, the former CWA president, became board chairman.

He laid out a series of priorities for the group, which included winning ballot initiatives at the state and municipal level, electing progressive candidates, and altering the makeup of the Democratic Party. The group focused on passing clean water legislation in the Upper Midwest; campaign finance reform in Howard County, Maryland; and building more affordable housing in communities around New England. And ultimately the Democratic National Committee adopted many of the groups' reforms, lessening the power of superdelegates, for example, and forbidding the party from playing anything other than the role of neutral arbiter in contested elections. Their efforts led to the biggest reforms of party infrastructure since the early 1970s and can be considered a real achievement of the group. Our Revolution made similar gains at the state and county party level, getting candidates to stand for party officers that are often left vacant and, in states like New York, changing state law to make it easier for citizens to vote, particularly in primaries.

But mostly what Our Revolution did was gather together some of the hundreds of thousands of people who had been inspired by and supportive of Sanders into some six hundred groups around the country. The cohort of dues-paying members grew to a quarter of a million people around the country, and the group's email list, estimated at five or six million strong, was the envy of the political world.

Power and money in the organization was centralized at headquarters, but decisions came from the local groups, which set the priorities for the national organization and threw themselves into wresting back power from Trump in the 2017 and 2018 elections.

Due to legal constraints, Sanders and Our Revolution were unable to coordinate. Local groups met with candidates and made endorsements, and then the national organization would screen them to see if they were worthy of carrying Our Revolution's imprimatur into the election season. If they passed, the national organization would help with money, ground troops, a robust social media presence, and campaign tools like personalized text messaging and emails. Still, the results were decidedly mixed.

In 2017, the group endorsed Tom Perriello, a progressive former congressman for governor of Virginia, but he lost in the primary. They declined to back the winner of that race, Ralph Northam, a former Republican who served as the Democratic lieutenant governor in the previous administration and who went on to win in the general election. Nor did they back Doug Jones, another centrist who won an upset victory against a Republican in an Alabama senate race, or Conor Lamb, who had a similar profile and ran a winning race for Congress in western Pennsylvania. Many of the progressives they did choose to back went on to lose, candidates like Dennis Kucinich, a former congressman and candidate for president who was running for governor of Ohio, and Daniel Biss, a state senator running for governor in Illinois. And many of the progressive favorites of that midterm season who did make it out of the primaries did so without Our Revolution's backing.

Ultimately, Our Revolution was something of a failure. It knew its goals—to create a multiracial social democracy and to pull American politics to the left, but beyond that, it couldn't quite figure out whether it was supposed to be a vehicle for Bernie Sanders's political ambitions or some kind of left faction of the Democratic Party. Entry for people who wanted to join the organization was nothing more than filling out an online form, and the local groups that joined in order to be part of a larger movement remained isolated from the central organization, which wanted them to act as affiliates of Our Revolution while the groups themselves wanted to act independently from national headquarters.

If there was an exception to this, it was in New York. There, hundreds of veteran volunteers from the campaign came together under the auspices of a new organization called the New York Progressive Action Network. They met in December 2016 in Manhattan and then again midway through 2017 in Albany.

Alexandria Ocasio-Cortez was there and she ran into Samelys López, who was also an organizer on the Sanders campaign and who invited her to come to a meeting of the Bronx Progressives, a new group that had formed from the remains of Bronx for Bernie after the 2016 campaign. The group had formed to keep the grassroots energy from 2016 flowing and hoped to challenge the local party apparatus in the Bronx, which was hidebound even by New York standards, keeping tight control over who could and could not get on the ballot and doling out patronage jobs to party insiders. "We wanted to create an alternative for people in the Bronx who felt like they weren't part of the local power structure," said López. "We wanted to create a space where, regardless of the issues or what party you belonged to or what your vision for the community was, you were welcomed. I know it sounds like an oxymoron, but we wanted to use politics as a way of building community. In campaigns you meet people you otherwise never would have met, and you form relationships with them, and it's a great thing to witness. Before her race, there were all of these people working in silos, but then we came together and it created this movement, this family that we are all a part of." (López, for example, became aware of the Democratic Socialists of America through the AOC campaign, later joined the group, and received their endorsement when she mounted her own failed run for Congress two years later.)

López was born in Puerto Rico to a Dominican mother and moved to New York as a child. She was in and out of the shelter system as a child but eventually made her way to Barnard College on a scholarship and later earned a master's degree in urban planning. Bronx Progressives used an urban planning approach to political organizing, utilizing a process known as "visioning"—getting everyone in a room to lay out their community's assets and come up with an idea for what they want to see in their home neighborhoods. López invited Ocasio-Cortez to come to some of these meetings, and Ocasio-Cortez did, later giving a short speech about her campaign. There was supposed to be a formal process for endorsements, but the group threw it out and decided to back Ocasio-Cortez almost immediately. "We just felt so aligned on the issues with her, that she understood our movement so well that we were like, 'You know what, we don't even need to have these meetings,'" recalled Randy Abreu, another leader of the group.

Abreu was a Bronx-born lawyer who had worked in President Obama's Department of Energy before returning to the Bronx and, unlike the rest of his peers in the administration, threw himself into the Bernie Sanders campaign. He eventually became a delegate at the 2016 Democratic National Committee and grew aghast at the way he perceived Sanders to be treated. He decided to run for the city council against a conservative Democrat and met Ocasio-Cortez when both candidates were invited to a career day at a local high school. They endorsed one another and campaigned together at parades in the Bronx. Abreu later went back to Washington, DC, to serve on Ocasio-Cortez's Capitol Hill staff.

After Ocasio-Cortez received the backing of the Bronx Progressives, word of the endorsement filtered up to the Our Revolution national chapter. Our Revolution's vetting document reveals how skeptically the national group viewed the race against Crowley. "Alexandria Ocasio-Cortez is a New York Times front page newsgetting Sanders-supporting candidate is [sic] taking on establishment Democratic Congressman Joe Crowley," the document read, and referred to an A1 story in the *New York Times* about female candidates who were shaking the walls of the Democratic establishment.

"I feel like I've been pulling punches," Ocasio-Cortez was quoted in the article saying over a text message to a group of her fellow Brand New Congress candidates. "Do you ever get any pushback from voters, or those who don't want 'party infighting'?"

"We're not trying to ask permission to get in the door," Ocasio-Cortez, added in the piece, which described her as an "organizer on Bernie Sanders' presidential campaign."

The vetting document—which was provided to me by a member of the group—went on to describe Crowley as "a co-sponsor of the Medicare-for-All Act, however, he takes a lot of corporate money" and as someone who "is very mainline establishment. Pure establishment and definitely a player, can be a bit of a bully. He claims to support now [Minnesota congressman Keith] Ellison's Single Payer Bill, but most people doubt his sincerity."

The document continued, stating, on the other hand,

> [Ocasio-Cortez] is a grassroots activist and as her website states "leader in her community." She is running on a platform of campaign reform, Medicare-for-All, a Universal Jobs Guarantee program, getting to 100% renewable energy, a federal student loan forgiveness program, and free tuition for public colleges and universities.

Alexandria Ocasio-Cortez is a third-generation Bronxite, educator, and organizer mounting a historic campaign for Congress in NY-14 (East Bronx, Northern Queens, Rikers Island). After growing up experiencing the reality of New York's rising income inequality, Ocasio-Cortez dedicated her life to education, organizing and activism, eventually mounting a 100% volunteer, no-corporate PAC effort to collect thousands of signatures and trigger the first NY-14 primary in almost a generation. As a member of a large Puerto Rican extended family, Ocasio grew up with a deep understanding of how one's zip code determines one's access to opportunity and economic well-being. After graduating from Boston University with degrees in Economics and International Relations, Ocasio worked in policy and education arenas while waiting tables to help her family keep afloat after her father's passing during the 2008 financial crisis. She understands working families and in Congress, she will fight for them.

The document noted that the winner of the primary needed approximately fifteen thousand votes in a two-way race. AOC ended up with just under sixteen thousand.

Bronx Progressives made a pitch for themselves too.

Bronx Progressives are made up of active advocates and organizers. We have seen and learned from elections of years and decades past. We live in one of the most disengaged communities in America (it is newsworthy around here whenever more than 15% of eligible voters turn out to vote). Our strategy is to utilize our own list of supporters within District 14's Bronx region. On top of this, we will aggressively meet voters where they are, in their homes; we will door-knock dense areas of the Bronx, particularly the Parkchester area which we have identified as a strong region of disengaged voters with potential to turn out 5,000 votes for Alexandria. Bronx Progressives voted unanimously to endorse and support Alexandria. To date, 9 members volunteered to help petition, and over twenty members are going to be trained on door-to-door canvassing and GOTV leading up to the June Primary. We will be efficient and strategic.

The report noted that Crowley had over $1.5 million in cash compared to Ocasio-Cortez's less than $50,000. This, plus the fact that Ocasio-Cortez was already a massive underdog, led the group to hedge on whether or not to recommend that Our Revolution endorse her candidacy; under the line for "staff recommendation," the report read: "No Recommendation."

It was not until three weeks before the election—after Nina Turner and other members of the group's leadership met with Ocasio-Cortez—that she finally received the backing from the person who had brought her into his political revolution.

"Alexandria is a working class New Yorker who is changing the face of what an elected official looks like," Turner said in a statement. "From waiting tables to educating children, she has seen firsthand how working families work more and more only to end up further behind."

The endorsement from the national group didn't amount to much, since the work was already being done on the ground, but it did give AOC a seal of approval from Team Sanders, and members did phone calling and texting on her behalf.

People for Bernie had fewer qualms. One of the founders of the organization, Kat Brezler, was a public school teacher in the Bronx and had run for the state senate, but she had seen her bid cut short when the local party in White Plains, New York, where she lived, endorsed her opponent during the party convention, leaving Brezler unable to get on the ballot.

Brezler was a veteran of the Occupy Movement as well, and early on in 2017 members of AOC's nascent campaign were reaching out for advice. Justice Democrats were tweeting at the People for Bernie account and asking for support. Brezler met up with Ocasio-Cortez at New York City mayor Bill de Blasio's annual State of the City address, this one at the Kings Theatre in Brooklyn.

Brezler was an invited guest and had an extra ticket that she held for Ocasio-Cortez. The two women, along with some fellow Occupiers, went out for beers at a local bar afterward and then for some late-night tacos. As much as AOC ran as an outsider, she knocked on the door of the power structure in New York City and State to the extent that she could. Brezler ran into Ocasio-Cortez again a few weeks later at the city council's Black, Latino, and Asian Caucus weekend in Albany, an annual event that is one of the signature networking events of the state governmental calendar. There, Brezler snapped a photo of Ocasio-Cortez cornering Ben Yee, an Obama campaign digital maven and fundraiser who in the years since started an organizing program that got thousands of New Yorkers involved in local politics. They ran into each other again at a protest in Lower Manhattan, and Brezler recommended some hires for the nascent campaign.

A few weeks later, People for Bernie endorsed Ocasio-Cortez, which led her to praise the group on Instagram as a "coalition that fights nonstop to make healthcare and secondary education accessible to EVERY American. Together we are a movement that understands our destinies are linked—and that a better America is possible for all of us." The group went to work for her, organizing its people to gather petitions and knock on doors.

But People for Bernie's main contribution to Ocasio-Cortez may have been blasting out her message online. The role of online organizing in politics is very much disputed. Social media, and Twitter specifically, tend to make a movement seem bigger than it actually is. The graveyard of political hopefuls is littered with candidates who seemed to have a throng of supporters online but couldn't activate that following in the streets. This seems to be changing though—not on Twitter so much as on Facebook—as more and more people use the social networking behemoth not just for sharing pictures of newborns but as their primary news source.

Soon after endorsing Ocasio-Cortez, Brezler stood with her on the streets of Corona where they livestreamed an interview on Facebook. They spoke of the difficulties of getting on the ballot, of and eclectic," noted NBC.com in its write-up of the event.[3] "Local artists brought puppets and dolls bearing resemblance to the 74-year-old self-proclaimed democratic socialist. Young students sat on blankets and huddled together as the night got cooler. The smell of marijuana wafted over parts of the crowd."

And one in that crowd was Alexandria Ocasio-Cortez, who, dressed in a purple suit festooned with Bernie buttons, gathered signatures for the campaign's digital outreach team.

"Bernie Sanders is the first presidential candidate to visit the Bronx since Robert F. Kennedy in 1968," Ocasio-Cortez wrote on Facebook on March 31, 2016. "His Bronx regional director told me yesterday that he himself chose this borough to open his NY campaign. This is a man who truly cares for working people—enough to make this community his first stop in New York.

"I'll be helping to head up today's volunteer data team at the rally, so let me know if you'll be around!" she added, inviting her extended social media network to follow along on her Snapchat page for regular updates from the rally.

But for Ocasio-Cortez, the race was also an introduction to New York's opaque election laws, revealing how the state laws are engineered to retain the incumbents and to fend off any challengers.

Not only does New York have a closed primary system, in which only registered party members may participate, but the state's deadline to register in party was nearly a year before Election Day, meaning that even as Sanders caught fire in the spring of 2016, many of his supporters found themselves locked out of the voting booth since they either were not registered to vote or did not belong to the Democratic Party.

But due to a screwup by New York City's inept (some argue, willfully inept) board of elections, many would-be voters couldn't exercise their franchise that year because they had been mistakenly knocked off the rolls. One of them was Ocasio-Cortez. She took to Reddit to explain what had happened to her.

"In shock right now—I've been a registered Democrat in NY for eight years and bussed myself four hours to my polling location in how the county party goes to court to knock off challengers in front of judges they have appointed. And Ocasio-Cortez laid out her case.

"New York 14 is the district where people start their American dream," she said. "Our district is half immigrant and it is one of the few communities in America where the American dream is not just an unreal or idealized thing, but you see it every day. . . . We have never been properly represented. Our district has changed so much in the last twenty years and we deserve to have that conversation and we deserve to have authentic leadership. People are so excited that the movement is here in Queens," she added. "We think of the movement sometimes in New York City as being more of a young hipster thing, and that's beautiful, but the movement is also here in Latino communities, in African American communities. This is a message for everybody."

Brezler couldn't help but kvell, telling Ocasio-Cortez, "There is something you said to me, that 'People have a bias about me until I open my mouth,' and that is you, it is you to a tee, and it is an honor and a privilege to watch."

Ocasio-Cortez has become one of the most skilled users of social media of our time, and on the People for Bernie interactions, you can see her learning how to do it. People for Bernie provided a hallelujah chorus for Ocasio-Cortez's tweets, which led her to play more to her audience. They dunked on reporters who were dismissive of her chances, and shot video of Ocasio-Cortez leading a Black Lives Matter chant in front of a Starbucks for the Queens Pride Parade.

By the end of the campaign, People for Bernie was borrowing an RV to park on the streets of the Bronx so that volunteers could avoid commute times when they were knocking on doors.

"I have been in a lot of campaigns, but there was something special about this one and something special about her," Brezler says. "I don't know if any of us thought she could win, but it seemed like there was something real happening on the streets, something that looked like a huge change that was taking over the country."

CHAPTER 4

THE LEFT OF
THE POSSIBLE

Star Trek.

That's what people remember most about Alexandria Ocasio-Cortez's acceptance speech after winning the endorsement of the New York chapter of the Democratic Socialists of America. DSA meetings include a constant stream of voting, vote counting conducted by hand, and sorting out the rules of parliamentary procedure, and while AOC spoke, other business was happening elsewhere, giving her free rein at the mic.

And so she talked about the Starfleet aboard the USS *Enterprise*.

The Ocasio-Cortez household didn't have cable when Alexandria was growing up, and so the channels came in staticky and scrambled. And so young Alex would sit on the floor and listen to what they said.

"I was obsessed," she confessed to the roomful of dozens of young socialist revolutionaries, pausing for a moment. "Stay with me. I promise you this is going somewhere."

Star Trek, Ocasio-Cortez told them, "was one of the most socially revolutionary shows on television." The actor who portrayed Lieutenant Uhura, Nichelle Nichols, was one of the rare Black women on television, and she was someone, Ocasio-Cortez told the group, who had considered leaving the series for a career on stage until she was talked out of such a move by Martin Luther King Jr. And, Ocasio-Cortez noted, Uhura was someone on the show "who wasn't in a subservient position but who was a leader."

"Watching this was one of the best little treats of my childhood. And the reason I bring this up is because one of the small, foundational aspects of that world, something that we almost take for granted when we're watching this is that when they think of a society a thousand years in the future, they think of a society that is intellectually, technologically and ethically advanced, a just society, where no one goes hungry, no one goes sick or homeless from lack of resources."

The young crowd loved it. *Star Trek*, the original series that Ocasio-Cortez was referring to, had gone off the air long before most of this crowd was born, but it had lived on in their childhoods through several different reboots and had played regularly on syndication in afternoons home from school. And here was some twenty-seven-year-old, speaking their language .

"And while that world may have been science fiction, the story was real and the show was real. And that value conveyed a powerful message—that ethical, advanced societies are not just wealthy, they are good." Ocasio-Cortez underscored, "And that is what we are here to establish, that is what brings us together: the pursuit of a good society, not just a rich society."

This was in many ways the core of AOC's message, and it is one that is unique to her and to her generation. It is talking about politics in language beyond material needs, beyond interest groups, beyond using the political system to get something for yourself.

"We come here together to advance the notion that the number one goal of an individual is not how many zeros are in . . . one's bank accounts," Ocasio-Cortez said, "but how many people are housed, how many people are fed, how much opportunity that every American has to pursue, what they can do to pursue self-realization, and that is what this is about."

There were some people in the Democratic Socialists of America who didn't want this fight. Joe Crowley, they said, was too powerful to be beaten. A socialist hadn't won a competitive election for Congress since Bernie Sanders in 1990. Better to focus on smaller, local elections, like in Chicago, where DSA had just elected a socialist alderman, or in Seattle, where Kshama Sawant had led an effort that created a fifteen-dollar minimum wage in the city.[1]

Alexandria Ocasio-Cortez had been showing up to DSA meetings in Queens, the Bronx, and throughout the city soon after she decided to run for Congress. It could seem a little craven—getting religion, or whatever the socialist equivalent is, just in time to embark on your political career—but few who were in any of those meetings felt that way.

"I mean, let's face it, everyone else there was pretty new too," said Sam Lewis, one of the leaders of New York DSA.

The Democratic Socialists of America had existed since 1982, when Michael Harrington, an activist and author, helped found the group with the writer Barbara Ehrenreich. For years, the group's membership had been minuscule, somewhere in the six thousand range, give or take. But membership exploded when Bernie Sanders ran as an out-and-proud democratic socialist in 2016, reaching ten thousand in November of that year and climbing to over fifty thousand in the months and years afterward.

Ocasio-Cortez was never an official card-carrying member, but soon after launching her campaign, she became a regular at the meetings, sitting quietly in the back, alone or with a campaign aide. For all the fear generated in the mainstream media that DSA was a group of crazed leftists about to turn American society Stalinist, their actual ambitions were far more modest, not something that even a committed conservative would likely disagree with, even if he would violently disagree with the means on getting there.

"A society in which you have healthcare for everybody, housing for everybody, enough food for everybody, anybody can have as much education as they want," said Frank Llewellyn, a founding member of DSA, a former national DSA president, and the treasurer of AOC's campaign.

In Llewellyn's formulation, there is no mention of destroying private property, liberating the proletariat, or nationalizing industries. There isn't even any talk of the plutocrats, or the millionaires and billionaires who have a stranglehold on our democracy, or the corporations looting the nation's wealth. It is a message more focused on lifting the bottom of the ladder upward than shrinking the top.

"Our goal is not to fix capitalism," he added. "It is to change capitalism into something else."

The Democratic Socialists of America grew out of the social tumults of both the 1960s, a time when left politics was on the march, and the 1970s, when those coalitions were shattering and the Left was facing a fallow period.

While most left-wing outfits in the United States come into being as a result of a splintering, DSA is the rare group that came out of a merger. It is one part New American Movement (NAM), which grew out of the disintegration of the 1960s radical campus outfit Students for a Democratic Society. By 1969, according to NAM cofounder Michael Lerner, it had grown from a "super-democratic, Martin-Luther King-Jr.-styled, nonviolent ('all we are saying is give peace a chance')" movement "into a violence-cheering and hateful group of people who were determined to tear down American society Malcolm-X-style: 'by any means necessary.'"[2]

NAM was slower to distance itself from Communism at the height of the Vietnam War than other left-wing groups at the time and less wedded to small-d democracy as a motivating virtue. But the group was committed to a grassroots theory of change, and it was focused on "revolutionary Democratic Socialist-feminism" and was further out front on issues of race, gender, reproductive choice, and sexuality than many of its allies were at the time.

Lerner wrote up the group's founding mission in *Ramparts* magazine, an organ of the New Left, and wanted his fellow leftists to "cease romanticizing the anti-imperialist and antiracist struggles that had led to a fawning acceptance of anything that came from nonwhite sources no matter how immoral or self-destructive."[3]

NAM, he said, should "become known as the sane voice of a progressive movement."[4] He called for states to withhold federal income taxes until the war in Vietnam was ended and demanded that the money go to education, child care, and healthcare.

"It was a way to put forward a different vision of the Left, moving away from the media's portrayal of us as violence-prone destroyers of society that the Weathermen leadership and the Black Panther Party had helped make a plausible picture to many," he wrote later in the essay. And it could have succeeded "had the rest of the Left backed it. But they did not. Instead, they denounced it as 'racist' because it was, they said, pandering to 'white skin privilege' by caring so much about certain white families and their concerns such as taxes, education, and health care costs."[5]

Lerner ended up leaving the organization soon after helping found it and eventually became a rabbi in Berkeley, California, where he founded the progressive magazine *Tikkun* and urged leftists and Jewish leftists, in particular, to put spiritual and humanistic concerns at the center of their politics.

The Democratic Socialist Organizing Committee, on the other hand, grew out of a crack-up of the old Socialist Party, which at its 1972 convention dropped the word "Party" from its name and became instead the "Social Democrats, USA."[6] The group no longer wanted to be known as a party in the political sense since it had long ceased competing meaningfully in national elections, and many among anti-Communist liberals who made up the group did not like that socialism had become increasingly seen as supporting the governments of Vietnam or China or the Soviet Union. Although the group had become associated with the New Left and campus activism, it retained some ties to the old labor left and the civil rights movement. Bayard Rustin served as the party's co-chair at the time of the name change—and it's almost entirely upper-middle-class youth faction urged the party to modernize by supporting seventy-eight-year-old AFL-CIO president George Meany for president in 1972.[7]

Much how Democrats were left wondering about their fraying ties to the white working class in the wake of Trump's victory in 2016, the Socialist Party at the time, and in particular its Young Socialist cadre, blamed Richard Nixon's 1972 win on the New Left takeover of George McGovern's campaign. In its convention that same year, the group's Young Socialist cadre, which the *New York Times* archly noted was "a convention with few blue collar delegates" released a platform that criticized the "upper middle-class youth who flamboyantly rejected 'materialism,' embraced voluntary 'poverty,' espoused oriental mysticism or more recently became 'Jesus freaks.'"

"Implicit in the 'counter-culture,'" the platform continued, "is a repudiation of the aspirations and struggles of ordinary working people."

This turn away from the radical politics of the New Left, and away from the term "socialism" and toward organized labor—which many leftists viewed as too transactional, bureaucratic, and, frankly, conservative—led Michael Harrington to leave the Socialist Party and start his own organization.

Harrington was by then one of the best-known socialists in the country, a journalist who had written *The Other America*, a deeply reported look at the nation's widespread, if hidden, poverty. The book helped put an end to the Eisenhower-era notion that America was a country that was increasingly prosperous and comfortable.

The book helped popularize the phrase "a culture of poverty," and Harrington argued that the poor in other countries had more in common with their American counterparts than they did with their own countrymen: they shared the same grinding lack of opportunity and lack of access to healthcare, education, and housing. Harrington went to Washington, DC, soon after the book was published, where he teamed up with Daniel Patrick Moynihan, then assistant secretary of labor and an old Greenwich Village drinking buddy, to write a report that urged a jobs program for the poor modeled on the Works Progress Administration, an idea that led to Lyndon Johnson's War on Poverty, even as Johnson changed the focus slightly into early childhood education and a stronger social safety net as a cheaper alternative.

After leaving the newly constituted Social Democrats, USA, Harrington, along with fellow journalist Barbara Ehrenreich, founded the Democratic Socialist Organizing Committee (DSOC). Their goal was to unite various strains of the Left so that antiwar and civil rights activists, feminists, and McGovern liberals could provide a vehicle to push the Democratic Party to the left. The group partnered with labor leaders and published a "Democratic Agenda," which was used to push for a commitment from Jimmy Carter to fight for full employment, an agenda item that his team resisted at the 1976 party convention. A resolution criticizing the Carter administration for not moving on the issue got 40 percent of the vote at the Democratic Party midterm convention, and DSOC was an early and enthusiastic supporter of Ted Kennedy's challenge to Carter for the Democratic nomination in 1980.

Delegates for the two groups met in Detroit in 1982, and, after some squabbling over how much to embrace the Communist world and their positions on Israel and Palestine, they decided to join forces to become the Democratic Socialists of America. With six thousand members, the DSA became the largest socialist organization in the country since the 1930s. Its goal was to work within the Democratic Party and become "the left wing of the possible," in Harrington's phrase, a nod to its core values of pushing the party while also being cognizant of political realities.

For much of the three and a half decades of DSA's existence, its membership was a fairly desultory affair. Membership never grew above ten thousand. The group competed, often unsuccessfully, with other socialist organizations to get a foothold on college campuses. There were just a handful of chapters around the country, and DSA's annual convention was often attended by just a couple of dozen comrades. David Duhalde, a former leader of the Young Democratic Socialists and a deputy director of the national organization, said that he would often duck out to work on his graduate school homework or to meet up with friends while conventions descended into a debate over whether the group should sell T-shirts or whether it should use the word "should" or "shall" in its resolutions.

There were some highlights. In the 1980s, a few members of Congress, most notably Ron Dellums of Oakland, counted themselves as members, as did David Dinkins, who would go on to serve one term as mayor of New York. After getting behind Walter Mondale in a "Stop Reagan" push in 1984, the group was an early and critical backer of Jesse Jackson's 1988 presidential bid. There were international conferences that occasionally garnered some press attention. Members were annoyed that the *Washington Post* covered one of their conventions but put it in the Lifestyle section, writing about how the group was trying to influence the Democratic Party. "The democratic socialists are preaching a new gradualist gospel which, in at least some important respects, isn't that far away from today's liberal establishment agenda," the paper wrote, noting that the group pushed for nationalized healthcare, the creation of a public energy company along the lines of the Tennessee Valley Authority, and a law that would require large corporations to notify the public when they raised prices. The story noted that the group pulled overwhelmingly from the white intellectual class and described how they eschewed pushing for Soviet-style command and control economies in favor of bringing more democracy into all matters of public life.

These proposals, the "cheerily disheveled" Harrington noted by way of defense against a cohort within the DSA that wanted further confrontation "may seem moderate to us, but they are radical to the nation."

The group's biggest foray into the electoral arena however was in 2006, when a little-known congressman from Vermont, someone who proudly called himself a democratic socialist even though he was not a member of DSA, decided to run for the Senate. The group rallied around Bernie Sanders in a way it had not for previous candidates for office, hosting a series of small-donor fundraisers that netted the campaign over $100,000, around 1 percent of the campaign's total fundraising—something that DSA members have pointed to with pride for years as evidence of how effective the group could be when it wanted to be. (The group also donated $500 to Ned Lamont, who ran as an anti–Iraq War candidate in Connecticut against Joe Lieberman in 2006; Lamont, who would go on to win the primary and lose the general election when Lieberman ran as a third-party candidate, returned the money.) Sanders also spoke at a DSA convention, an event that doubled as a fundraiser for his campaign and that brought 125 people to the DSA's annual convention, far more than would have attended otherwise.

In the 2000s, though, the group did not get behind any candidates for local or federal offices, and none sought their endorsement since doing so would have meant being immediately labeled a fringe candidate. Socialism, much as it was in the 1980s, was in retreat, as even avowed Socialist parties in Europe were embracing austerity in the wake of the post-2008 economic downtown. DSA had only one full-time staffer, its executive director, Maria Svart, who took over after Llewellyn stepped down, and the group began focusing on getting recognized just by the larger left universe, hoping for coverage in magazines like *The Nation* and *In These Times* and to get invited to left-wing and labor forums and conventions.

This didn't change much even as Sanders became a political phenom in 2015 and 2016. DSA membership remained around 6,500, even as the group tried to recruit Sanders into the race and then quickly glommed their movement onto his with a series of "We Need Bernie" fundraisers and events that used the campaign to talk about the Democratic Socialists of America and what Sanders and their distinct brand of socialism would mean in the US. A number of DSA members served as delegates at the Democratic National Convention in Philadelphia, and the national political press began to call, asking what this little-known group was all about.

By election night 2016, DSA's membership had increased from just over six thousand to just over eight thousand.[8] The group was laying out plans to use its modest increase in clout to push for some of Sanders's goals in a Clinton administration—universal healthcare, increased taxation on the wealthy, and a reform of the financial services industry.

Instead, on the night of November 8, 2016, the world changed. Donald Trump was elected president, and distraught Democrats were wondering what went wrong and, more importantly, what to do next. The day after the election one thousand people joined the Democratic Socialists of America, and the day after that the sign-ups were in the hundreds. As "Bernie Woulda Won" began to trend on Twitter, a group that was once fighting for respectability was suddenly central to the debate about how the Democratic Party saw itself. On Inauguration Day, another thousand joined.

It would not be until months after the Trump inauguration that DSA achieved something close to respectability in left circles and became something of a force in Democratic politics. After his loss, Sanders wrote a book to rally his supporters and to earn more money on a book tour. The first printing of *Our Revolution: A Future to Believe In* included a shout-out to Progressive Democrats of America (PDA), a group formed in the wake of the 2004 election by Howard Dean and Dennis Kucinich. That group was a who's who of progressive leaders, featuring people like Jesse Jackson, Barbara Lee, and Medea Benjamin on its board, but it had long ceased to have much relevance for the activists who powered the Sanders race. He didn't mention the Democratic Socialists of America at all in his book. In the book's second printing, several months later, however, PDA got dropped and DSA was at last given a mention.

AOC did a similar dance. She had been attending DSA meetings in the Bronx/Upper Manhattan branch after the election but hadn't connected with the group much. Vigie Ramos Rios, who had just been hired as Ocasio-Cortez's campaign manager, convinced her to check out some meetings in Queens.

"I don't think she felt at home with them," Ramos Rios reflected. "It was much more of an Upper Manhattan feel than a Bronx feel over there, and she was from the Bronx. Queens wasn't a red diaper baby kind of place where you had to know about Marx and Trotsky. In Queens you didn't talk about semantic arguments. It was an old union kind of a space."

Ocasio-Cortez joined the group in February 2018, soon after Ramos Rios took her to her first meeting in Queens, but she was never the type to add a red rose to her Twitter handle. (The red rose, a symbol of democratic socialism in the US ever since the "bread *and* roses" demands of textile labor unionists in the early twentieth century became ubiquitous among some corners of social media after the 2016 election.) It was Ramos Rios, in fact, who put the phrase "democratic socialist" on Ocasio-Cortez's website, something she did without AOC's knowledge. The group around AOC would grow to regret it in the heat of the campaign and after she won, as it became a kind of shorthand for AOC's beliefs and for her political affiliation, when neither was exactly true.

"In terms of her belief systems, she was already there, she was already a democratic socialist," said Ramos Rios. "But she was very aware of her district, and her district, like a lot of districts, people were just waking up to this. When you are talking to the average voter, they are not talking about Marxism or democratic socialism. They want to know, 'What's a vision of the future I can actually believe in?' That's where she was all along, even when I first met her. If she had any discomfort with it, it was with the idea that if you bring regular voters in here they wouldn't feel like they belonged."

Susan Kang, a Queens activist who was an early supporter of the Ocasio-Cortez campaign, agrees. "She never presented herself as DSA," she said. "It was something the media put on her because to call someone socialist is splashy, it's sexy, in a way that calling them a 'Justice Democrat' is not, especially back then, because no one knew what a Justice Democrat was, anyway. AOC was given the label by the media, and frankly she was kind of shocked by it."

It would be tempting to imagine that AOC joined DSA as a way to ingratiate herself to a politically powerful force that could provide her with ground troops to dethrone Crowley. But it is not the case. When Ocasio-Cortez started going to meetings, DSA was scarcely engaged in electoral politics at all. Some members felt that engaging in electoral politics, in fact, ran counter to the mission of the group, that politics was inherently corrupting. Portions of the group thought it better to engage in building a grassroots movement that was outside of the political process.

But in 2017, the Brooklyn chapter of DSA got behind the city council campaign of Jabari Brisport, a public school teacher who was—contrary to Harrington's original directive to operate within the confines of the Democratic Party—running on the Green Party line against incumbent Laurie Cumbo, a favorite of the Brooklyn establishment. Running in a general election, Brisport got 29 percent of the vote. The race hardly merited much attention, but if political observers were paying attention they would have seen that a new force had come into being.

"You are running a grassroots campaign, you're looking for anybody who's willing to endorse outside of the current political system. And that's the thing DSA had going for it. It wasn't a big powerhouse, especially in Queens, and especially in the Bronx, but it was a group of people, some of whom actually lived in her district, who were willing to buck the state Democratic Party, the Queens and Bronx Democratic Parties, that weren't afraid of getting their asses handed to them," said Ramos Rios.

How Ramos Rios came to be involved with the group is not typical. Like so many others, she joined DSA after the election of Trump, but she was in her forties, a generation older than many who joined then, and she had a marketing career in the financial services and insurance industries. She was politically interested but not engaged, and then she got sick and had to declare bankruptcy in order to qualify for Medicaid.

"I was always on the leading edge of technology," she said. "I worked in customer service in the banking system. And on the phone, I'm on the Internet, and I'm crying because I need Medicaid and I can't figure out how to make it happen. And that moment crystallized something for me: if this is what I am experiencing, what is this like for people with less time, less resources, less education?"

Ramos Rios heard about Bernie Sanders not from a twenty-something, but from her seventy-something mother, who was familiar with Sanders's work on veterans affairs in Vermont. She started volunteering for the campaign, and it turned out that she was an organizing wizard and eventually became a Sanders delegate. She joined DSA after the Trump election because senior members of the New York DSA asked her to; there was suddenly a lot of interest in the group, and someone with Ramos Rios's skills could make the group cohere.

The experience of Aaron Taube and DSA is more typical. He grew to be a key component in Ocasio-Cortez's campaign, but he didn't even identify as a socialist or a democratic socialist before joining the group.

"Trump's election was a traumatic event for so many people, and all I could think of was that things are going to get really bad," he said. "There was this far right, Fascist force gaining power in the country and where was the Democratic Party? They were nowhere."

And so Taube showed up to his first DSA meeting the day after Trump had been elected. There had been efforts by groups affiliated with the local Democratic Party to get young people—Taube was twenty-seven at the time—to join them but those efforts were ad hoc and seemed limited to election season. Taube was struck upon entering a DSA meeting in late 2016 how well-organized the group was. After his very first meeting, there was an orientation session that spelled out the fundamental precepts of democratic socialism; the meeting ended with everyone banding together and singing "Solidarity Forever."

"There was this sense, from the start, that you are in this and this is what we are about and that you are in this thing together," he said.

A few months later, Taube and a few other members of the Queens DSA were invited to a small get-together for Ocasio-Cortez in a Jackson Heights apartment.

"I couldn't believe just what an incredible candidate she was. She had this way of explaining the intersectional nature of racism and of classism, and she communicated just a real frustration with the way things are and a belief that things could be better," Taube remembers.

Once he left, it seemed obvious that DSA needed to get behind her in a big way: "This was a person who was very, very good at this. She is going to steamroll this guy. You have this dynamic young person with great politics and a great vision, and she is up against this mediocre long-term elected official? She is going to be the first socialist elected to Congress, the youngest woman elected, easy."

Taube and some other members went to meet with members of the Brooklyn chapter of the DSA, who had been around the party longer and who had more experience in electoral politics. They told Taube and the Queens members that they absolutely should try to get Ocasio-Cortez the DSA endorsement, but that they should also know that her chance of victory was nil.

Taube said:

I remember them saying, "Go ahead, this is going to be a great exercise for Queens DSA. You are going to learn how to do an election. You are going to learn how to run a canvass. You are going to build new leaders. But just so you know, Joe Crowley is going to have the support of every local elected official in the district, he's going to have a ton of money, and this is worth doing

because you are going to make the county machine easier to beat
in the future, and it is going to be great to talk about the failings
of the Democratic Party in Queens, but just know that you are
going to lose."

Despite Ocasio-Cortez's poor chances of winning, Taube went
about attempting to secure the DSA's endorsement of her, which
was no easy task. The difficulty he faced speaks to one of the challenges DSA has if it hopes to become a political force.

AOC had wanted DSA's help to gather signatures to get on the
ballot. She had noticed that the group always seemed to be present at events around the district, including rallies and community
organizing meetings. The group, however, wasn't prepared to help
with petitioning, so a few members volunteered their time, making
it clear they were on their own and not as a part of DSA. At the
time, DSA had never won anything in New York or anywhere else
for that matter, but getting their endorsement amounted to a Sisy-
phean task for Taube and the campaign. He had to win not just one
DSA endorsement, but three: the Upper Manhattan Bronx branch,
the Queens branch, and NYC-DSA.

There was skepticism. Some of it was that DSA would waste
whatever momentum it had had from the losing Brisport city council race the year before, especially considering AOC was such a long
shot. There were concerns that she wasn't officially calling herself
a socialist or a democratic socialist, that she wasn't sufficiently supportive of the Boycott, Divestment, and Sanctions movement that
pressured Israel to comply with international law, and that "we are
going to get our asses kicked, really bad, and we don't want to put
in our members' time for something that isn't going to work," Kang
remembers. "We are trying to fight for socialism. That takes a lot
of time."

Taube, however, went about whipping votes at DSA meetings
across the city to get the group to endorse Ocasio-Cortez. He made
a hardball politics pitch, something that would have been familiar
to any regular in the Queens County Democratic Party aware of the

ethnic and tribal politics of New York City: DSA had a reputation as a mostly white, mostly male, mostly privileged group. Here was a Latina from the Bronx, a bartender, who wanted to carry their banner. Win or lose, it would help dispel some of the group's "Bernie Bro" reputation.

"I would tell them we have this amazing left candidate who would be a great representative of our organization," Taube said. "The DSA has a reputation of being a bunch of white dudes. It's getting better, but some of that is fair, and we have this amazing, dynamic Latina running against the worst person in Queens politics. It is exactly the kind of contrast we want as far as what kind of organization we have."

Plus, Taube said, "we needed a campaign. Queens DSA needed something to rally around to help us get off the ground. I would tell people, 'You may have concerns about her ideological purity or about whether or not we can win, but that this was going to be very good for the long term health of Queens DSA.' It's not like we had very much to lose."

The endorsement process of DSA couldn't be more different from the endorsement process of most labor unions and civic organizations. With DSA, a small group or even a single individual will typically meet with all the candidates, give (or not) the organization's imprimatur for use on palm cards and campaign literature, and maybe provide a few ground troops to go door knocking.

For DSA, by contrast, the promise of an endorsement meant an engaged group of supporters who would knock on doors, stand on street corners, and pass out palm cards because they believed in the candidate's cause.

"That is our theory—that a union cannot mobilize the way they used to because these decisions are made in a top-down kind of way. They endorse candidates for transactional reasons as much as ideological. And DSA members can look at this race and say we have this amazing, inspiring candidate and we participated in the decision to support her every step of the way," said Taube.

As Taube whipped votes, he stayed in touch with the campaign, and AOC also went to DSA meetings to make her pitch, exciting members when she came out for abolishing ICE and when she said housing was a human right. It is hard to imagine the hoops she had to go through for a DSA endorsement, as compared to others, but in the end it was worth it.

And, indeed, had there been other options, she may have foregone the whole thing. But even like-minded local political clubs and social service organizations that saw themselves as counter to the Queens Democratic Party wouldn't endorse her; her chances of winning were so slender that the risks of getting on the wrong side of Crowley, who was likely to be the next Speaker of the House, were just too great.

Even DSA members concede that the group's processes can seem opaque at best and maddening at worst. In the summer of 2019, roughly one thousand DSA delegates gathered in Atlanta for their annual convention. It took most of the first day of the convention for the group to settle on their bylaws going forward—these bylaws were not for the coming years or even the next quarter, but rather for the three days of the convention.

The convention came at a fraught time in the group's history. Trump was denouncing socialism daily, mainstream Democrats were distancing themselves from the label (even the Georgia Democratic Party had issued a statement asking DSA to stay away), Bernie Sanders was polling near the top of the Democratic field, and Elizabeth Warren was just beginning her surge. Pro-Trump MAGA protesters were encamped in front of the Westin Peachtree Plaza, one of Atlanta's few union hotels, where they were waving American flags, holding Trump signs, and warning that socialism—free college, healthcare for all, and a Green New Deal—would never be allowed in America or in Atlanta. That weekend, there had been a pair of mass shootings, one in El Paso, which killed twenty-two people, and, that same night, one in Dayton, Ohio, which killed ten. It was hard to escape the feeling that the convention at the Westin, which was guarded by just a single DSA member checking badges, could be a target.

DSA conventions are easily mockable, as a thousand people in a conference room raise their arms and wiggle their fingers to signal agreement, to avoid offending comrades sensitive to sensory overload. In addition, speakers are admonished for using the gendered term "guys" and measures are proposed and seconded only to be voted down by countermeasures, all involving the group's internal structuring.

It is all in a belief that in order to make the change they want to see in the outside world, DSA must, within its own systems and processes, recreate the world as they would like it to be.

"Our goal is to build a mass movement of people in communities all over the country, organized in their neighborhoods and their workplaces and in the political arena to force landlords and bosses to stop exploiting people," Maria Svart told me in Atlanta. "To force politicians or to elect our own politicians to pass policy reforms that transform the power relationship between the poor and working class and the capitalist class. And ultimately we want to change our entire economy and our society so that we don't have children going to bed hungry every night. We don't think that a society that allows that to happen is an egalitarian society."

The growth of DSA over the last few years has been remarkable. It isn't just AOC, or Rashida Tlaib or Ilhan Omar, her fellow members of the Squad who also call themselves democratic socialists. There are nearly one hundred DSA members elected to local offices all over the country, most notably in Chicago, where a half dozen alderman were serving in 2019 and where they pushed for more housing affordability, increased rent control, and more community oversight of the police. There are democratic socialists in the Maryland legislature and in the city councils of Denver, Philadelphia, and Seattle.

"You may not know this, but we in the South have been waiting for you," Khalid Kamau told DSA members on the opening day of their 2019 convention. Kamau is a democratic socialist and a city councilman in South Fulton, Georgia, which is 90 percent African American. He stood before the group to tell them that they weren't just welcome in the South but that they were welcome in communities of color believed to be hostile to them.

Kamau told the group that their problem is an "electability complex," a belief that the American people shy away from candidates who call themselves democratic socialists.

"The people in this room are going to destroy the electability complex," he announced. "And let me tell you how: We are going to run candidates. And we are going to win. Today's fringe is tomorrow's future. While you are here, I need you to dream your biggest dreams so that we can win the future."

CHAPTER 5

THE CIVIL WAR TO COME

The founders of Brand New Congress lived in different cities spread across the country, and so conducted their business on weekly conference calls. And on one of them in early 2017, Isra Allison was almost trembling with excitement. The organization had been together for about a year and had been sifting through hundreds of applications seeking their endorsement for what was an audacious project: to run congressional candidates in each of the 435 congressional districts in the United States. Allison—who had worked in mid-management for Duke Energy in Charlotte, North Carolina, before dropping everything in 2016 to volunteer for Bernie Sanders and who had since become Brand New Congress's executive director—told the group, "This nomination is amazing. We have to go out and meet her."

The application was from Ocasio-Cortez's brother, Gabriel, and it told AOC's story: her journey from the Bronx to the suburbs, the financial aid that allowed her to attend Boston University, coming home after her father died, and helping support her family, and her political awakening with the Sanders campaign.

Allison arranged a phone call, and the two ended up connecting as Ocasio-Cortez was coming back from the Dakota Access Pipeline protests on the Standing Rock reservation in South Dakota. If they were interested in her before, now the leaders of Brand New Congress were hooked.

"Other people in her position, I don't want to say 'sold out,' but they could have gone and done something more high-paying, and she went back and tried to serve her community," observed Alexandra Rojas, one of the founders of Brand New Congress. "It wasn't about checking a box on issues, it was about their experiences, what prepares them to go into a room where there are four hundred people telling you to do something you don't think you should do."

But if Brand New Congress wanted to hear Ocasio-Cortez tell her story to them, she wanted Brand New Congress to tell their story to her. How was this whole process going to work? How would she support herself if she ran a quixotic campaign against one of the most powerful people in Washington? And if she won, then what? Could she do more good running for local office?

"Convincing people to go and scream into the void is very, very difficult," Rojas said. "And if you are a woman, running for office can really fucking suck. It just doesn't seem like something you can do, and so we told her, and we told all of our candidates that they aren't going to be alone, that we are building a movement."

It seems certain that Alexandria Ocasio-Cortez would not be in the United States House of Representatives were it not for Brand New Congress. It was the group that first recognized her preternatural political abilities and provided the early infrastructure and support—without which she would not have even been able to come close to mounting a viable run against Joe Crowley.

The group owes its existence to the Bernie Sanders campaign. Corbin Trent grew up and was living in Morristown, Tennessee, in the foothills of the Smoky Mountains and deep in the heart of Appalachia, for generations a symbol of a kind of grinding white rural poverty. His grandfather and his father owned a metal and woodworking business. Trent took it over when he was in his twenties, but the business went belly-up. He then moved to Upstate New York to attend the Culinary Institute of America. After earning his degree, he moved back home and opened a food truck called Crazy Good Burgers. The truck eventually burned in a fire, and he raised money for another, but that caught fire too. When the Sanders campaign took off, Trent, who had no political experience and not much political interest, signed up as a volunteer, eventually becoming the head of the campaign's distributed organizing arm.

Distributed organizing differs from the traditional approach of hiring paid canvassers to go door to door, a top-down system that relies on a substantial budget and a willing workforce. It also differs from the more volunteer-driven style of making signs and holding bake sales, which most campaigns rely on. Instead, distributed organizing focuses on ceding central control, allowing activists at the local level—and who know their communities best—to take charge in their neighborhoods. While there is a chance that strategy can go awry as local activists lose interest or forge a path outside of the campaign's values, it can also encourage would-be organizers to take on larger roles and make them feel as if they have an important role in a campaign that could be headquartered hundreds of miles away.

Trent teamed up with Zack Exley, who had joined the Sanders campaign after a career in politics. In 2000, Exley had been furious that George W. Bush wouldn't own up to his past drug use—Bush said he had "grown up" in the years since—while still pushing for harsh penalties for drug felons. Exley achieved some renown at that time by creating a series of satirical websites, including GWBush.com, which featured a doctored image of the then Texas governor sniffing lines of coke and ran fake news releases, among them one that alleged that Bush had pardoned all the drug felons in Texas prisons because they had "grown up" too. Bush called for the website to be taken down, saying there should be limits on free speech, which naturally led to even more traffic. Exley went on to work for MoveOn and for the Howard Dean and John Kerry campaigns before teaming up with Sanders. Exley and Trent ended up traveling around the country hosting a series of "Bernstormers" with Sanders supporters, while the campaign focused almost exclusively on the four early states. At these gatherings, the duo would talk about what

Sanders wanted to do as president and then solicit volunteers to host phone banks, canvasses, and the like, getting people to sign up for shifts before they could walk out the door.

Eventually, it became clear that Sanders was not going to win. Exley, with his long experience in left politics, wanted to create something that resembled the parliamentary system of European countries, in which lawmakers ran as a slate, putting forth a unified platform of what they hoped to do in office. The US parties, as Exley saw it, had become indistinguishable from each other. If you favored fiscal rectitude, for example, did you vote for Republicans, who were supposed to be the party of balanced budgets, or for Democrats, who actually paid attention to deficits once they were in office? There is a divide on social issues like abortion and gay marriage, but how often do Democrats push on those issues when they get into power? And why is no party talking about, let alone meaningfully addressing, widening inequality and stagnating wages?

"Look at it from the perspective of a working-class person in America," Exley said. "Does either party have something to offer where they say, 'Here is our project, here is what we are going to do to turn around the American economy'? The answer is no. In fact, if anything, it's the Republicans because they at least say we are going to cut your taxes so you can keep more of your money. Ask any Democratic politician except Bernie what they would do to turn the economy around and it is just a mishmash of little policies."

Brand New Congress, as Exley saw it, would run a slate of candidates proposing a WPA-style mobilization to boost the economy, sending millions of Americans to work on critical infrastructure needs. And he had seen with MoveOn, and then with the Howard Dean campaign and later the Barack Obama campaign, how a big idea could excite millions of people to donate their time and money, and that the mechanism for doing so was no longer reliant on big-money donors or establishment players. The only question was whether such an effort could be applied to remake Congress. Exley started asking around at the Sanders headquarters to see if anyone was interested, but most of the young staffers were planning on jobs in the nonprofit or think tank worlds and were not interested in Exley's grandiose visions.

Apart from Trent, however, two young organizers were interested: Saikat Chakrabarti, a Bay area software engineer and entrepreneur, and Alexandra Rojas, a community college dropout from California by way of Connecticut. They all figured that Hillary Clinton was going to be the next president. But how could they harness the energy of the Sanders political revolution in a real and tangible way in Washington, knowing that his political career was likely over?

The answer was audacious and, truth be told, a little bit nuts. What they came up with was a plan to run against every single member of the House, all 435 of them—Democrat, Republican, independent, it didn't matter. What did matter was the candidates came from outside the political class. Nurses, teachers, social workers, accountants—anyone with a desire to serve but who didn't think politics was for them, ideally someone who was already considered a leader in their community. "Extraordinary ordinary people" is how the group described their ideal candidate.

"The kind of people that we wanted to run were people who actually had skill and experience in running some part of our society, whether they were a nurse or a teacher or a foreman in a factory, all kinds of people," Exley told me. "People who are good in their field and who are respected and who were really servants of their communities. People who put their communities ahead of themselves and where they had had chances to sell out and hadn't. I always thought about the factory owner in Vermont or New Hampshire whose factory burns down and who instead of rebuilding in China may rebuild here even though it's not going to mean the highest profits for them, or the teacher who stood up to their administration and to the union to look out for the interest of their kids, or the principal who just really went to the mat to fix their school. We would literally cold call these folks and say, would you, will you run for Congress."

They called the group Brand New Congress, and their plan was to put an all-call out for nominations, select from the best of them in each district, and then to centralize all of the infrastructure of the various campaigns into a single Brand New Congress headquarters. This way the campaigns would not have to come up with 435 different field strategies or hire 435 different spokespeople or fundraising consultants; the candidates could focus on talking to voters, and the politics would be handled by the pros.

By running as a single entity, the organizers behind Brand New Congress also were shrewdly cognizant of a reality of American politics, that presidential campaigns have a galvanizing and catalytic effect on the nation's popular imagination. Congressional races, not so much, and so the organizers behind Brand New Congress aimed to change that. Running 435 different congressional races, they hoped, would meld 435 separate stories into one that would capture the public's attention in the same way that Hillary versus Bernie had or in the way that Hillary versus Trump would a few months later.

The only hitch was—or, rather, one among several hitches was—that most congressional districts have nothing like the diversity of party or ideology that the nation as a whole does. More and more Americans tend to live in clusters of like-minded sorts. But when they don't, congressional gerrymandering slices districts in such a way that most incumbents never face a serious challenger, especially not in the general election. (In the early decades of the twenty-first century, reelection rates for sitting members of Congress have never sunk below 85 percent and have often been well above that percentage, even as a series of wave elections has swept the majority party out of power repeatedly during that time.)[1] And the founders of Brand New Congress were all Bernie Sanders–style progressive Democrats.

Aware that carrying a D next to your name in roughly half the congressional districts in America is a political scarlet letter, Brand New Congress decided that if they were serious about replacing the sitting Congress with one closer to the needs of the people, they would need to run in Republican primaries as well as Democratic ones.

The decision to compete on Republican turf was also due to the fact that many of the founders came from Republican territory, places like Appalachia and south Texas and the forgotten mill towns of New England, areas liberal cultural values did not have much appeal. And their experience on the Sanders campaign led them to believe that a new political moment was in the offing. Sanders's success was due not just to his success at rallying the left wing of the Democratic Party but to his appeal to independents and even some Republicans.

"What we noticed as we were going around the country talking to volunteers and voters and supporters was that, first, there were a lot of independents, people who were agnostic politically, that were inspired by the Sanders campaign," Trent told *In These Times*. "It's not hard to get people to run [as Republicans], so much, as getting Republicans to vote for the people who are running on [our platform]. I think you do it by accentuating the connections that we have across the aisle. It's going to be the desire to have high-wage jobs, a growing economy, access to affordable healthcare, access to good education. I think that what conservatives and Democrats and independents want is very similar. They want their lives to be better and their kids' lives to be better." And so, as Democrats convened on a sweltering weekend in Philadelphia to officially nominate Hillary Clinton, the leaders of Brand New Congress began touring the country, meeting mostly with people they had met through canvassing during the Sanders campaign to sell the idea of a Brand New Congress, raising money along the way to extend their journey further and staying at the "BernBnB," their nickname for the network of spare couches that Sanders supporters lent to one another as they found themselves in strange cities to fight for their cause. They got the word out however they could, going on MSNBC, hosting Facebook live chats, and talking with podcast hosts and any interested reporters they could find.

They ended up with twelve thousand applicants, and after an intensive screening process, just thirty-one candidates received the official Brand New Congress endorsement. It was far from the four hundred they originally envisioned, or even the fifty they thought they could reach, but it was a start.

One of those was Robb Ryerse. He was a fundamentalist pastor who had had a crisis of faith, and so in his late thirties he moved his family to northwest Arkansas, where he started a new church more in keeping with his values. It was the day of Trump's inauguration, and Ryerse was adrift as he tried to sort through what to do with his life in the new America. His wife was listening to a podcast hosted by Rob Bell, another one-time evangelical preacher whose crisis of faith had led him to question the concept of Hell. Bell was talking to Exley about Brand New Congress. Ryerse's wife handed him her phone so he could listen, and although he had never been involved in politics before, the idea struck a nerve, and he started talking to all of his friends about the group. Soon enough, they nominated him.

"It really appealed to me that Brand New Congress was post-partisan, recognizing that the two-party system and the party establishment of both parties care more about their own power and keeping their own power than they do about solving the biggest problems we face as a country," Ryerse said. "And the idea of trying to subvert that system by running Republicans in bright red districts and Democrats in deep blue districts seemed like a way to work within the two-party system to subvert it. It's a strategy that just made a lot of sense. And the other thing that was really appealing is the idea of running regular people, not career politicians, but regular people who aren't gonna take corporate PAC money so that their loyalty can be with the voters who sent them to Washington."

Despite the group's best intentions, Ryerse was the only Republican to go through the screening process and run as a Brand New Congress–endorsed candidate. Running as a Republican was a necessity, he says, in his conservative Arkansas district, one represented in 2018 by Steve Womack, a Tea Party Republican who defended Donald Trump's efforts to restrict immigration from non-

European nations, saying that "people from countries that are behind the times, depraved countries," would have trouble to "actually fit into the society as we know it."[2] Womack also questioned the
science of climate change[3] and suggested that a rise in gun violence
was due to a proliferation of single-parent households.[4]

Ryerse calls himself a "progressive Republican," someone in the
tradition of Dwight Eisenhower or former New York City mayor
John Lindsay in a party that was previously taken over by conservatives and has since been overrun with Trumpists.

Ryerse noted that political parties change, and he had to decide if he wanted to leave the Republican Party or stay and offer
an alternative voice. Ryerse said, "I know it's an uphill battle, but
the historic values of the Republican Party are much more progressive than people realize. It was a Republican who was president
the last time we had comprehensive immigration reform. It was a
Republican president who created the Environmental Protection
Agency. It was a Republican president who coined the phrase 'the
military industrial complex.' Within the Republican Party, there's
this strand of really progressive ideas, and I'm trying to tease that
out, that there is a vast difference between Republican leadership
and Republican voters. Republican leaders are way out of step with
Republican voters."

Running for office, especially for a first-time outsider matched
up against an entrenched incumbent, can be a daunting and dizzy-
ing experience, and so Brand New Congress attempted to make it
easier for their candidates by trying to get them to cohere as a group,
figuring that if some of them did make it to Washington, they could
serve as a quasi-caucus and use the strength in their numbers to
fend off lobbyists, fundraising needs, and the other corrupting influ-
ences in the nation's capital.

And so Brand New Congress held a series of organizing sessions
with their chosen candidates in Knoxville, Tennessee, and in Washington, DC, and over the Facetime app where they traded tips and
built out the Brand New Congress platform. Ryerse met Ocasio-
Cortez at one of the first sessions in Knoxville, when there were just

a handful of candidates in the program. They were seated next to each other and signed the paperwork to start their campaigns alongside one another. Afterward, Ryerse came home and told his wife, "I think I met the future president of the United States."

"I had never met anyone so charismatic," he said. "There is this notion that you see in the conservative media that she is just this clueless bartender, and I found it to not be the case at all. She came across right away as smart, articulate, and incredibly willing to hustle."

Brand New Congress picked up on something that has long been a feature of American society and politics but that has been supercharged in the last couple of decades: a belief that amateurs know as much as experienced professionals about how to get things done. It is why the guy who builds a mainframe computer in his garage on weekends is lauded as a hero, but the person who slowly climbs up the ranks of IBM is forgotten about. In politics, it has been axiomatic that the nation's wisdom lies not in Washington but out among "the people," and long experience in legislative chambers is a hindrance, not a help, to gaining higher office. No one embodies this more than Donald Trump, the first person to hold the presidency without having spent a day in politics or the military, but Barack Obama's almost straight ascent from the Illinois legislature to the White House also embodies this, as do the anti-Washington campaigns of George W. Bush and Bill Clinton.

And it makes sense in this current moment that an outsider would be appealing—when so little has changed in the nation even as the party in power has changed frequently and Congress and most of official Washington live cosseted from the rest of the country (members of Congress earn more than 88 percent of American households[5]). Brand New Congress was based on this very idea, and AOC embodied and articulated it.

"The great divide in the country isn't between left and right," she told the group at their retreat in Tennessee, a line she would use over and over again on the trail. It is "between those that have power and those that don't."

According to Isra Allison, it was AOC who, coming from her poor urban district, steered the Brand New Congress platform toward issues important to the Bronx and Queens, particularly toward criminal justice reform and the environment, issues that became the Green New Deal.

"We aren't going to be able to outspend our opponents," AOC told the group, another line that she would use over and over again in the months afterward. "But we can out-organize them."

Ryerse and AOC developed a friendship, as did the rest of the slate. He texted her on the night of her debate with Crowley: "Go kick his ass," which led her to write back, "Don't worry, I will," and they remained in touch throughout the campaign.

By that time, Ryerse had already lost his race, getting just 16 percent, or approximately nine thousand votes against Womack. It wasn't a surprise. Soon after he became an official candidate, however, Ryerse came to realize that the early promise of what it meant to be a Brand New Congress candidate was not going to be borne out. The money and the excitement, which the new venture was supposed to inspire in the electorate, failed to materialize, and thirty of the thirty-one Brand New Congress candidates went down to defeat. The infrastructure never materialized either, in part because candidates balked at sending their money to a central organization and in part because local political operatives on the ground knew better.

"One of the most difficult parts of campaigning was shifting from this vision that we bought into and then the reality turned out to be very different. And that shift was, was tough because I had no plans to run for office. This was not the trajectory of my life," Ryerse said.

Looking at the period of 2016 through the 2018 midterms, Brand New Congress may look like something that was invented in the intoxicating romance of a galvanizing presidential campaign, that, once viewed again in the sobering light of dawn, can seem kind of crazy. It is hard to find nonpolitical people who want to, and are capable of, running for Congress. And people are generally satisfied with their local elected officials, even as they give low marks to Congress as a whole. And to the extent people want a brand-new Congress, they almost always want to kick out the people from the other party and almost never want to replace the representatives from their side with a crop of largely unknown people with no experience in government.

But life trajectories have a funny way of surprising. Isra Allison stepped down from Brand New Congress in 2019 in order to become the campaign manager for Cori Bush, a progressive who in 2020 unseated William Lacy Clay, a longtime incumbent from St. Louis in an Ocasio-Cortez/Crowley-sized upset. Ryerse, after the washout of his own race, stepped in as Allison's replacement.

After 2018, Brand New Congress reoriented, downsizing their previous ambitions to do a wholesale takeover of the House of Representatives and instead focusing on what they could and could not do to help their chosen candidates be successful. In 2020, the group ran no Republicans, an admission that party identification and ideology pretty much trumps everything else in American politics in our era, but still helped lend their seal of approval to some remarkable upsets by left-wing challengers to establishment Democrats. But recognizing that different parts of the country may have different ideas about how best to achieve progressive ends, the group now does not come up with a unified platform, but instead has a "21st Century Bill of Rights," which lists broad themes, and not Sanders-inspired ways to get there, including, "Every American has a right to quality of life" and "a high quality education is essential to secure the rights of life, liberty and the pursuit of happiness."

"It's a recognition that there are some shared values that our candidates have," said Ryerse. "And we also recognize that they express those values and express them in policy positions that may look a little bit different district to district. We have things we believe in, like affordable healthcare for all and a Green New Deal, and we aren't shy about that, but we have made a shift away from strict policy positions for our candidates to shared values."

Brand New Congress's visibility soared after the release of *Knock Down the House*, a documentary from filmmakers Rachel Lears and Robin Blotnick, who chronicled the campaigns of four Brand New Congress candidates but spent the bulk of its narrative on Ocasio-Cortez's campaign, since she was the only one to have won. After the movie was released, a flood of volunteers reached out to join the group, more than they were capable of handling. "People saw that movie and they realized they wanted someone like Alex as their representative, and we are here to help them get that," Ryerse said.

Brand New Congress endorsed nearly forty candidates in 2020, an improvement over the thirty-one they backed in 2018, and the organization serves as a kind of public utility for these candidates, helping out where needed. If the candidates are unfamiliar with how to handle the press, Brand New Congress connects them with another candidate or another contact who has experience in that area. They still get the whole slate together and have regular video conference calls.

"We're providing training for them and it's everything from policy to strategy to personal care, self-care, and personal coaching and how to deal with the emotional ups and downs of being a candidate," Ryerse said. "We're there to help these grassroots candidates with the types of things that if they had millions of dollars and could hire consultants to do these things, they would."

Allison said the mission of Brand New Congress remains the same—"to repeal and replace Congress"—but it is hard to know how much of a future the group could have. It was created in a moment when it was widely assumed that Hillary Clinton would be president, and that a recalcitrant Congress—roughly divided between Republicans and Democrats and secure in the knowledge that few people in their districts could credibly challenge them— would work to maintain the status quo. The world that Brand New Congress woke up to in 2017 was highly partisan and remained so for the next three years. In that world, there could be no compromise with the other side, and the public mood was for sobriety and experience in lawmakers to counter the chaos coming from the White House.

"We're trying to build something long-term," said Ryerse. "We know our particular brand of post-partisanship may not play well in a 'Blue No Matter Who' kind of political environment that has been caused by Trump. But Trump isn't going to last forever, and we are going to keep working to have regular people represent us in Congress."

One such candidate is Lauren Ashcraft. A former JPMorgan Chase project manager turned comedian turned democratic socialist, she decided to follow AOC's path two years later and run against Carolyn Maloney, a twenty-seven-year incumbent who represented a district centered around Manhattan's East Side. She had been nominated by someone in her community and gone through several rounds of interviews with the leaders of Brand New Congress to test her viability in a race in which several contenders were lining up to challenge the incumbent in an environment where candidates around the country were running as "the next AOC."

"They want to make sure that we are running on a message that they support as well," Ashcraft said. "They don't want candidates who take corporate PAC money or who don't want to get money out of politics. They want people-powered grassroots candidates."

Brand New Congress asked about Ashcraft's background, her staff, how the campaign was going, and what she knew of some of the other BNC candidates. And once Ashcraft was chosen, she met up with other BNC candidates in Washington, DC, where they talked about fundraising and where experts like Andres Bernal, a former foreign policy adviser to AOC, briefed them on economics and answered questions. There was not much provided, however, in the way of a campaign infrastructure. There was no help with polling, a text program, or advice on how to run a canvassing operation across a diffuse district. Candidates were mostly on their own, but they were not alone.

"Knowing that people are going through the same thing and you can reach out and ask them questions, that's been one of the most valuable things of being a part of BNC," Ashcraft said. "And also just being there to support each other, because it's definitely not easy to be a progressive candidate going against people who've been in office for decades. But doing it as a coalition and supporting each other and knowing that we believe the same thing is really helpful." Ashcraft ended up coming in third place with 13 percent of the vote.

By the time the 2018 election season was under way in earnest, the four founders of Brand New Congress had come to see the mission was going to fail. Most of the hundreds of community leaders they reached out to in order to convince them to run for Congress politely declined, not believing the promises of this new group's vision of politics. Once it became clear that it was only a couple of dozen candidates, rather than four hundred or so, Exley, by his own admission, lost interest, and the other three founders—Rojas, Chakrabarti, and Trent—came to realize they needed a more targeted approach.

In the course of the campaign, the group had come to know Cenk Uygur, the founder of the Young Turks online television network and host of *The Young Turks* show, and Kyle Kulinski, a left-wing political commentator who hosted his own show on the Young Turks called *Secular Talk*, which melded progressive politics with an atheistic worldview. Uygur ended up leaving the group when a series of misogynistic blog posts came out (see chapter 6), and Kulinski served in a more advisory capacity, but Rojas, Chakrabarti, and Trent along with Waleed Shahid, an organizer with the Working Families Party—an umbrella organization of left-wing and labor groups that had its origins in the backlash to the Democrats' turn toward the center under Bill Clinton in the 1990s—decided to spin off what they had learned from BNC and start their own organization.

They called their new group Justice Democrats, and their mission was much easier to understand than the mission of Brand New Congress. Instead of focusing on every single House seat, they would zero in on just a handful of Democratic incumbents. It was an effort that drew resemblances to the Tea Party, which had given the Republican establishment fits during the Obama era by knocking off incumbent after incumbent and replacing them with fire-breathing radicals who often went on to lose to Democrats in the general election.

But whereas the Tea Party cost the Republicans their congressional majorities in the Obama era, Justice Democrats decided to focus only on Democrats who were in safe seats, so that regardless of who won the primary a Democrat would retain the seat. The group focused on Democrats who they believed were out of step politically with their districts—Democrats who were too moderate, too focused on raising Wall Street cash, and too ensconced by decades of incumbency in Washington to be attuned to the needs of the people. But it was not just ideology that mattered to Justice Democrats; it was also identity and representation. Many white, older, and more moderate members of Congress, they believed, represented districts deep in America's urban core, which had grown increasingly diverse over the last couple of decades. Incumbents managed to hold on year after year mainly because no one bothered to challenge them, and Justice Democrats vowed to change that.

And they had another innovation that shook up the sclerotic world of political strategy. Most organizations on the right and on the left keep a close tally on who they endorse and who they do not. Groups want their imprimatur to mean something, and they want politicians to fight over their support. It is how clout grows in Washington, DC, and it is why, after every election, groups as varied as the National Rifle Association and Democracy for America send reporters a scorecard of how their endorsed candidates did. Since the groups want to be with winners, these tallies can look like the win-loss record of the heavyweight champion of the world, with more than a hundred victories to just a handful of defeats.

Justice Democrats decided to do something different. They would put all their chips on long shots with the belief that if even one of them could get through, it would alter the power dynamic of US politics. Although they tacitly supported dozens of candidates, they actively recruited twelve and gave them most of their attention and expertise, including Kaniela Ing in Hawaii; Kerri Harris of Delaware, who was running for the US Senate; and Abdul El-Sayed, who was running for governor of Michigan. If even one went on to win, they figured, it would shake loose the power structure of the establishment, a bet that turned out to be right.

"It's remarkable," said Adam Green, a cofounder of the Progressive Change Campaign Committee, which started a decade ago as a liberal alternative to what it saw as its stodgy counterparts in Washington. "Everybody is so concerned about clout and about relationships, and they have no relationships, so they just go for it, taking big chances. They pick fights that would be high-risk, high-reward for others that are low-risk, high-reward for them. And if they are successful on just a fraction of them, it gives momentum to all progressives."

The Justice Democrats platform was not so different from that of Brand New Congress, but it was sharper than Brand New Congress's "transpartisan" politics could allow for. Justice Democrats called for a Green New Deal, a federal jobs guarantee, the abolition of ICE, a pledge to not take any money from corporate PACs, and—as an absolutely nonnegotiable baseline—support for Medicare for All.

But, for a long time, Justice Democrats looked like they would end up a failure as well. By the end of 2017, they had no money, and the media seemed consumed by Donald Trump and other new progressive groups like Swing Left and Run for Something. None of their candidates looked like they had much of a chance of winning, and the one who had the best chance, Alexandria Ocasio-Cortez, was growing tired of her own campaign, which was looking increasingly quixotic. She had begun to tell friends that she was thinking of getting out of the race.

The group knew they had something special in AOC from the start. "The thing that struck me about her from the beginning, to be honest with you, is that she just seemed actually kind of *normal*," recalled Zack Exley. "She is supposed to be this super-lefty, but she doesn't present as a super, wacky lefty. She just presents as this normal person, but compared to all the dead fish who are in Congress it means she comes across as something extraordinary."

As winter turned to spring, AOC decided to stick it out, however. Shahid, who had for a while been the sole Justice Democrat staffer working on the race, convinced the group that they should pull up stakes elsewhere and go all in for AOC. The original vision of some four hundred candidates had been whittled down to twelve, and now it was going to be further whittled down to one.

"I was really frustrated because I saw a lack of priorities where they were giving all the candidates the same amount of energy and time and resources," recalled Shahid. "And I thought that there was one person here who seems way better than all the other ones. We did a strategic planning retreat where I said to the group, 'What is our goal here? We have twelve candidates who we have recruited, all of whom have no money and no exposure. What are we trying to do here?' And they all said we really want to unseat someone. So if that's the point, then pick one. Because we are going to fail. We have no money. We have little staff. And I said we should pick AOC because she was the best candidate we had, and there was serious activist energy around her."

And so they did. Corbin Trent moved to New York and started sleeping on Saikat Chakrabarti's couch, and Alexandra Rojas moved to New York as well, and what had been a slightly shaggy campaign operation began operating on all cylinders.

Shahid had grown up in an apolitical family in Virginia suburbs of Washington, DC. His parents emigrated from Pakistan. His father took a job as a garage attendant, eventually rising to oversee a string of garages as part of a company that manages parking lots, and his mom worked in local public schools. Shahid was ten years old on 9/11, and when his mother picked up him and his two siblings early from school that day, they found the highway home blocked off as the police prevented commuters from traveling into DC. They were just a few hundred feet from their home, but police wouldn't let them go any farther, and Shahid's mother and one of the officers started getting into an argument, with her pointing out that they just needed to get off the highway to get home. Eventually, the cop pointed a gun at her, while the three kids in the back started screaming and crying, pleading with her to turn around.

She did, driving forty-five minutes out of their way to get home, and when they eventually got there, Shahid's mother organized a vigil on their lawn for the whole neighborhood, as they still awaited word from people who lived nearby and who worked at the Pentagon. "I remember everyone—white, Black, Latino, gay, all of these people we had never met before because who knows your neighbors—holding American flags and singing the national anthem. I didn't even know my mother knew the national anthem," said Shahid.

Shahid had a cousin who had overstayed a visa and had been tipped off to authorities because he had said disparaging things pre-9/11 about George W. Bush to his coworkers, which led federal authorities to come to his workplace for questioning. Afterward, Shahid's parents warned him not to discuss politics at school.

And so, as young people do, he started discussing politics at school, eventually organizing a school walkout as Congress debated immigration reform in the Bush years. It was the height of the real-estate boom, and Shahid's father invested his retirement savings in a second home that would be used to generate some extra income. Then the housing bust happened, and everything they owned was lost. Shahid got a full ride to Haverford College, an elite school outside of Philadelphia, where a classmate of his one summer went to go work for Dave Brat, an obscure economics professor at Randolph Macon College in Virginia. Brat was mounting a long-shot campaign against Eric Cantor, then the Republican House Majority Leader and someone thought to be the next Speaker of the House, and made Cantor's support of comprehensive immigration reform the most central issue in the race.

In one of the biggest political upsets in generations—until AOC's, at least—Brat won, and afterward a headline in *Politico* said "Cantor Loss Kills Immigration Reform."[6]

"It was just one fucking race!" Shahid said. "One fucking race and immigration reform was dead."

As the 2016 primary got underway, Shahid was working at an immigrants' rights legal aid group in Philadelphia; people would come in—asylum seekers, undocumented immigrants—and Shahid recalls telling them, day after day, to just keep watching CNN because Obama was bound to pass something sooner or later that would clarify their legal status.

"It was the most demoralizing, uninspiring time of my life," he said. Disappointed with Obama, Shahid got a job with the Working Families Party, which supported Sanders. After the 2016 election, he wanted to figure out how to make systemic changes in politics, or "culture shifts"—not just winning arguments, but changing the terms of the whole debate.

"The idea is that you bring moral questions to the public's attention, and have the public rally around it," Shahid says. "Reframe the issue so that the choices are stark, and let the public decide rather than people in power." He points to how the "99 percent" became a buzzword after Occupy Wall Street; how Obama and Hillary Clinton eventually came to oppose the Keystone Pipeline after supporting it; how "Abolish ICE" quickly went from a fringy Twitter slogan to one embraced by mainstream Democrats. Either you favor ripping kids from their homes, or you don't. And if you don't, suddenly the policy choices aren't incremental: they're rather stark.

Alex Rojas's trajectory to the group was different, but equally telling in terms of what it reveals about the kind of person who becomes a leader in this new movement.

Rojas had grown up outside of Hartford, Connecticut, one of the few students of color in her high school class. Her father was a first-generation American whose parents emigrated from Peru, and her mother emigrated from Colombia. She wanted to go to college in California and so moved west with the hopes of establishing residency and racking up a few community college credits in the meantime.

In order to make ends meet, Rojas worked three jobs in retail while attending classes. She didn't know anyone at school, so she decided to join student government in order to make friends. Soon she was leading protests against the school administration for attempting to limit the number of evening and morning classes students could take. Meanwhile, the state of California changed the residency requirements to receive in-state tuition, which meant Rojas's whole plan fell through. Around this same time, someone sent her a video of Bernie Sanders's 2015 campaign kickoff speech on Lake Champlain, where the Vermont senator railed against the millionaire and billionaire class for rigging America's economy and its democracy and called for a political revolution to beat it back.

Rojas was transfixed. "He had a very clear analysis of how we got here as a country: special interests have bought our politicians and that the only way that we're going to get things done and fix big problems is by running on big ideas. And we need a movement and we need millions of people that are typically disengaged to stand up and demand it and take it back," she recalled. "And he said we are not going to get this done because we have to go up against the fossil fuel industry, the pharmaceutical industry, this multibillion-dollar lobbying operation and it made me feel like I could be a part of changing history."

Rojas started organizing for Sanders at community colleges in southern California, and through that met senior figures from the campaign who offered her an unpaid internship in Burlington, Vermont, provided she could get there herself. And so she got in the car and drove east, her California experiment over. She joined the Bernie campaign with Chakrabarti, Exley, Trent, and others. Then she joined Brand New Congress and Justice Democrats when it was clear a new mission was needed.

It can seem odd after the election of Trump to think that the problem with American politics was with the Democratic Party. It was the Republicans, after all, who had rallied around Trump despite previously warning of the dangers he posed to the nation. It was the Republican majority in the Senate who had kept a Supreme Court seat open and who now threatened to pack the court with a conservative majority. It seemed like a natural moment to rally around the Democratic flag, but that is not how the nascent Justice Democrats saw the moment.

"After the election, was I mad at Donald Trump? I guess, kinda," said Uygur. "But mainly I was mad at the Democratic Party for blowing it. How could you lose to this guy?

"I came to realize Democrats are never going to learn," he went on, "and that the only way to make a difference is to defeat the corrupt corporate Democrats. They get paid to lose. The corporate donor pays them to be weak, and pays Republicans to be strong."

Rojas saw things the same way.

"Healthcare, police brutality, climate change," she said. "All of these we have known my entire lifetime that they are a problem and politicians do nothing about it. I have never lived a moment in my life and probably my children either where this country won't be at war.

"And seeing that, the assessment that I've come to is that it's not just Republican leadership that has failed. It has been Democratic leadership that has been stagnant on these issues too. And if we are not fighting with every ounce of our being for everybody with policies that match the scale, scope, and urgency of the problems that we're facing, it's a disservice to the next generation. And I think it makes political sense if every representative from a blue district is actually fighting for Democratic values. We are trying to bring out the best in Democrats so that we can defeat the worst in Republicans."

The goal of Justice Democrats isn't to replace the entire Democratic Party—it is to move a suite of progressive agenda items closer to reality, policies like a Green New Deal, Medicare for All, and an end to the war on drugs. And primarying sitting members, they find, is the best way to make that goal a reality. The great secret of Justice Democrats is that of their recruited candidates, only AOC won, but AOC's win helped shake the world and made those policy priorities many steps closer to reality than they would have been if Justice Democrats had just played it safe and focused on adding to the Democrats' majority in Congress.

Many activist Democrats have come to believe over the last couple of decades that somewhere deep inside the Republican Party apparatus, decency still abides. It is a belief that the true Republican Party isn't the party of Donald Trump, Mitch McConnell, or even George W. Bush and Dick Cheney. Those Democrats believe that were it not for its rightest most fringe—those Tea Partiers and evangelicals and moral values voters—the GOP would come in good faith to negotiate with Democrats.

Justice Democrats take a different view. There is a radical fringe all right, a minority that controls the agenda of an entire national political party, and that keeps the nation from achieving a measure of economic justice. But, according to Saikat Chakrabarti, "It's the radical conservatives in the Democratic Party. That's who we need to counter. It's the same across any number of issues—pay-as-you-go, free college, 'Medicare for All.' These are all enormously popular in the party, but they don't pass because of the radical conservatives who are holding the party hostage."

Declaring war on the Democratic Party establishment is an easy thing to do when you are outside of the tent. It is much harder to do from inside, to look your colleagues in the eye and tell them they need to be replaced. And it is doubly hard to then ask them for their support on a piece of legislation. Such guerrilla tactics, sitting members targeting their fellow partisans, was unheard of.

But Justice Dems say they don't care. These are crucial times. They compare it to the Civil War, when the Radical Republicans similarly attempted to purge the party and heal the nation.

"There is going to be a war within the party," said Shahid. "We are going to lean into it."[7]

CHAPTER 6

THE STORYTELLERS

Sam Lewis is a union and tenant organizer who joined the Democratic Socialists of America soon after the 2016 election, when pretty much everyone else did, and he quickly developed a reputation as one of the New York chapter's savvier thinkers and strategists around electoral politics.

Lewis grew up in in Brooklyn to liberal parents, then went to Oberlin College and became chair of the College Democrats. He volunteered in Washington State for congressional candidate Darcy Burner, a fierce opponent of the Iraq War and a favorite of the nascent Netroots—an online group of progressives who try to pull the party leftward—but who ultimately lost. Lewis wrote his senior thesis on the Employee Free Choice Act, a priority for organized labor in the early years of the Obama administration. The law, often known as "Card Check," would have made it easier for workers to join unions, and Obama scored key union endorsements after promising to sign it during the 2008 campaign. He never did though, despite having a majority in the House of Representative and a filibuster-proof majority in the Senate. Watching it all left Lewis confused and disillusioned.

"There were things I just thought we all agreed on, like we all agreed that ending poverty was the right thing to do and a priority," he told me. "And if we can't do it, it is because there are

Republicans, and they stop it. But then you volunteer for a couple of campaigns, and you realize that's not the case, that there are Democrats who wouldn't cut out corporate interests from the party even if they could."

The rest of the early Obama years were dispiriting—a mixture of more military interventions abroad, bank bailouts, millions of Americans losing their homes and their jobs in the midst of the Great Recession, and no accountability for any of the people who made it possible. Lewis got a job working on the Fight for $15 campaign, which aimed to raise the wages of low-income fast-food service workers across the country, and checked out Occupy Wall Street in Zuccotti Park. There were walkouts, petition drives, strikes, and rallies, but what really put the campaign in overdrive was when Kshama Sawant, an avowed socialist, was elected to the Seattle City Council on a pledge to bring a fifteen-dollar minimum wage there. Less than a year later, the higher wage was city law.

Inspired, Lewis left his job and started going to Socialist Alternative and International Socialist Organization meetings, two militant Trotskyist organizations that were then running on life support, the handful of members in each organization already collecting Social Security benefits and squabbling among themselves. He quickly grew disheartened. Lewis then heard about Jacobin, and its reading groups, and decided to give those a try.

"It was incredible. You would see eighty or ninety socialists in a basement in Brooklyn on a Monday night. I wasn't even in DSA at the time, but I was like, 'Wow these people are doing something! If we wanted to, we could start winning city council races just with this group here.'"

This was precisely what the reading groups were designed to do. They were the brainchild, of a sort, of Neal Meyer, a doctoral candidate in sociology at New York University. Meyer had been involved in campus activism while an undergrad at Harvard University, working on organizing the university's low-wage employees. He joined DSA soon after graduation, hoping to find an outlet to continue his activism.

He, too, was dismayed by what he saw in the pre-Trump era of DSA, a group with just a couple of dozen committed dues-paying members. At some meetings, he and the only other person under fifty-five were considered "the youth faction," and meetings would devolve into arguments about socialism in China and other arcana. The activism mostly consisted of people showing up at picket lines with handmade signs, often tied together sandwich board–style with twine. "It felt very marginal," Meyer recalled. "It was sort of embarrassing."

Meyer eventually got hired by DSA to serve as a full-time student organizer and started going around the country trying to get young people to join the group. And he was struck by how difficult it was. "To them, socialism, I don't know, it just felt kind of old. It was the twenty-first century, and it just didn't seem relevant to people."

Jacobin magazine had been started in 2010 by Bhaskar Sunkara as a hip, well-designed and well-written update on some of the dour lefty magazines of old like *Dissent* and *In These Times*, and in just a couple of years had become a sensation with the Left, with a circulation of ten thousand.

Reading groups, organized by the readers of left magazines like *The Nation* and *Mother Jones*, are not a new idea. "Discussion groups," usually listed in the classifieds—back when magazines had them—were held in living rooms in the liberal enclaves of Berkeley Hills and Boulder, Colorado, going back years. These were largely sparsely attended and genteel discussions over tea, but Meyer and Sunkara wanted to do something dynamic and figure out a way to supercharge what they sensed was a new energy crackling among the young after Occupy Wall Street. As they were discussing what to do next, Jacobin reading groups had sprung up on their own in Boston and Washington, DC.

"They were just getting together once a month and discussing articles, and there was this energy and excitement about them that you weren't even seeing at DSA meetings," said Meyer. "They had maybe ten to fifteen people under the age of thirty-five, but they somehow felt alive."

And so Sunkara hired Meyer at *Jacobin* to serve as a part-time circulation manager and organizer in charge of setting up a nation-wide reading group program.

"We wanted to popularize socialist ideas," Meyer said. "The goal was to deepen the political education work of the magazine and actually get people in person to meet and argue about these ideas and really test out their hypotheses with each other and figure out what differences they had, what questions they wanted to learn more about."

And part of the point, too, was that if you got a bunch of left activists together, they would start to recognize that they could truly have power, could move an agenda forward, and could win local and, maybe even bigger, elections. This was a change in approach from the activism of Occupy Wall Street a few years before. As Sunkara and Meyer figured, for years the Left had been energized by spontaneous, anarchic demonstrations and mobilizations and had eschewed the basic building blocks of political power like organization and leadership. "There was this assumption that politicians and that people in power were people of good conscience and morals and that if you protest loudly enough they would just change course," Meyer said.

Although the meetings were a bunch of people sitting around and talking about what they read, they weren't about only people sitting around and talking about what they read. They were about what to do outside of the room where they were gathered, how to get further involved, and how to make the ideas discussed a reality. Meyer wasn't even aware that other liberal magazines held reading groups, but that wouldn't have mattered anyway.

"It's the difference between socialism and liberalism," said Meyer. "Socialism is about inspiring people to make enormous sacrifices in their lives, to participate in this big political project they can't make money off of. It's going to cost them. It is going to cost them a lot of free time. Their partners' parents might think they are crazy. So it's a different project to tie yourself to, but it is also more exciting and more inspiring."

Meyer had never organized anything in his life when *Jacobin* put out an email to its subscribers asking if they would like to start a group; four hundred people wrote back, expressing enthusiasm. Meyer set up phone calls with all of them, and later he and Sunkara put together a syllabus that included articles to read from the most recent issue *Jacobin* and a few outside articles and otherwise allowed people to organize their time as they saw fit.

At their peak, the *Jacobin* reading groups were in forty American cities and a few more abroad, including one in Kathmandu, Nepal. Meyer estimates there were probably around two thousand people who came through them at one time or another, a more impressive figure when you consider there were only six thousand members of the Democratic Socialists of America at the time and probably only a few hundred active members.

The meetings that Meyer organized took place at the Brooklyn Free School, a nontraditional private school in the Fort Greene neighborhood. Participants, which sometimes numbered sixty to eighty people, would mingle for a bit and then break off into small groups for discussions. There would be the occasional cranks from the Spartacus League who would come and denounce DSA as a bunch of revisionists who had Rosa Luxemburg murdered in Weimar Germany, and when they could, the group's leaders would invite members of labor unions to share what they were going through, but for the most part the meetings were filled with young people making connections and learning about the cause.

"A lot of left meetings at that time, there were like the same five people plus one poor new guy who stumbled in and couldn't figure out why everybody was arguing about Trotsky," said Meyer. At *Jacobin* meetings, on the other hand, "there was this sense of energy about them. People were just excited there were that many people in a room."

Afterward, the group would spill out for beers at Hot Bird, a beloved Brooklyn bar filled with picnic tables around a fire pit that has since been demolished to make way for a twenty-nine-story condo complex. One among that group was Julia Salazar, then just a twenty-four-year-old Columbia graduate from Miami who had moved to the rapidly gentrifying neighborhood of Bushwick after graduation.

Salazar had been involved with campus politics and activism, and when she graduated, she missed the heady, intellectual discussions in her Columbia classes. At one of the meetings, someone brought up the idea of volunteering for Debbie Medina, a democratic socialist running for the state senate. Salazar scarcely considered herself a socialist at the time but remembered "seeing other young people volunteering on the campaign, and other young socialists, and all of these people who were coming together around an idea, and then acting to achieve that idea. It was a very vivid moment for me."

Thanks to the reading groups, Salazar ended up joining DSA, and though Medina went on to lose her election in 2016, two years later, with a newly emboldened DSA behind, Salazar ran for the same seat and—boosted by a key endorsement from AOC—won handily.

By that point, the energy behind *Jacobin* reading groups had begun to fizzle, but it didn't matter to Meyer and Sunkara. The young radicals were already at home in the mothership of DSA, and their work was done.

But even if the reading groups had never existed, it would be impossible to overstate the impact that *Jacobin* magazine had on creating the political moment that Ocasio-Cortez was a part of. The magazine was started by Sunkara when he was an undergraduate at George Washington University. Sunkara's parents are Trinidadians of Indian ancestry; they moved to the upper-middle class New York City suburb of Pleasantville with their four children, and Bhaskar was born a year later, the only natural-born American of the bunch.

His parents worked long hours, and so young Bhaskar spent a lot of time at the local public library, where he discovered George Orwell, and later Trotsky, and then other Marxists in a random reading program that, he says, could just as easily have introduced him to Ayn Rand and Edmund Burke. Bhaskar became aware of how an accident of birth—he was born in America while his four siblings were not—afforded him opportunities not available to them.

By the time Sunkara was a teenager, he had joined DSA.[1] In college, he got sick and had to take time off, and during that time he delved even deeper into Marxist texts and history. That's when he got the idea to start *Jacobin*, announcing in its opening pages a desire to both change the world and to have a sense of style while doing it.

"Publications with tiny audiences have a knack for mighty pro-nouncements. A grandiloquent opening, some platitudes about 'resurrecting intellectual discourse' followed by issue after issue of the same old shit. We can admire the confidence of our peers, but there is something pathological about this trend," Sunkara wrote, pledging that this venture would aspire to avoid the traps of lefty publications that had gone before, which he placed in two camps: "the esoteric ones, sites of deliberate obfuscation, utterly discon-nected from reality" and those that are "unchallenging rags that treat their readers like imbeciles. With mainstream pretenses, high school yearbook prose, and rosy reports of mass movements in the making, their role is even more disorienting."[2]

"Substantive engagement does not preclude entertainment," he went on. "Discarding stale phrases and ideas does not necessitate avoiding thought itself. Voicing discontent with the trappings of late capitalism does not mean we can't grapple with culture at both aesthetic and political levels. Sober analysis of the present and criti-cisms of the Left does not mean accommodation to the status quo."[3]

Other than AOC, there is perhaps no figure who has come to embody the new socialist left quite like Sunkara. He is, to put it mildly, a force of nature, the kind of person who can either meet you right now or as soon as he gets back from a talk he is giving in Santiago or Vienna. Twice he canceled interviews with me at the last minute, once because he had forgotten that he was scheduled to a radio debate with Whole Foods CEO (and noted libertarian) John Mackey and another time because he had to prep for an interview with the former president of Ecuador, Rafael Correa. Eventually, he told me to meet him at the Verso Loft, where the half-century-old lefty publisher keeps its headquarters in a large open space looking out on the Brooklyn side of the Manhattan Bridge.

It was a Friday, the first cold night of the winter, and *Jacobin* was hosting a panel discussion featuring an Internet talk show host, a Princeton historian, and the host of *The Hill*'s web-only streaming morning talk show on the state of Bernie Sanders's 2020 presidential campaign. But there were easily two hundred people there, very few of whom seemed older than thirty-five, sipping cheap red wine and five-dollar Stella Artois. Sunkara was a whirlwind of activity, talking with fans, tending bar, and setting up extra chairs once it became clear that there were more people coming than expected.

"This kind of thing is about building brand relevance. I figure if people are going to go to political events they might as well be our own," he told me. Unlike other outlets that have to spend money to promote their events, *Jacobin* merely puts the word out on Twitter, sends a couple of email blasts, and the crowd appears.

"We want to harden social bonds. It is helpful for our overall project if people feel like they are part of a collective project that is beyond their own individual social media accounts on the Internet," he said.

Sunkara said that if he had been a savvier businessman, he would have noticed that something was happening with the magazine he started in his dorm room, something that would come to fruition during the activism and organizing of the Sanders campaign and then in the Trump era. *Jacobin*'s subscriber base was rising by 40 percent a year in 2013, 2014, and 2015.

But Sunkara is as savvy a businessman as they come, someone who can quote year-over-year subscription rates, bulk mailing costs, and who, according to *Jacobin* managing editor Micah Uetricht, is most comfortable while negotiating shrink-wrap rates for polyurethane bags with their industrial shipping supplier.

"I think he is one of the most unique figures in the history of the American Left," Uetricht said. "It's this classic, son-of-immigrants business success story of someone who used his business savvy to create a socialist empire that, to be clear, is not lucrative in the least."

Uetricht bounced around the Midwest as a child and young adult. His father was a pastor in a Lutheran church, and sometime in high school, Uetricht came to fancy himself a radical activist, interested in anarchism, veganism, dumpster diving, and black-clad protests in Seattle in the late '90s and Occupy Wall Street a decade later.

But he grew tired of the look when he read Saul Alinsky's *Rules for Radicals.* "If the real radical finds that having long hair sets up psychological barriers to communication and organization," Alinsky wrote, "he cuts his hair."

So Uetricht cut his hair and got a job working at a newsstand at the Chicago airport, trekking hours there on the bus back and forth surreptitiously organizing the workers there while the bosses weren't looking. After leaving that job, he started writing for *In These Times,* another publication of the Old Left. There, he met Sunkara, who was also writing for the publication while trying to get *Jacobin* off the ground. Sunkara worked in an administrative back office at the City University of New York, where, in between stapling course packets together, Sunkara put together the magazine.

The sensibility of *Jacobin* was a rejection of much of the liberal magazine publishing world that had come before. The issues were gorgeous. One of Sunkara's first hires was graphic designer Remeike Forbes, and the sensibility was, on the one hand, open hearted and, on the other, as sharp as a spear. They argue for a Left that isn't hung up on using the right labels to describe things or calling people out if their liberalism isn't sufficiently pure, but that actually works to form coalitions.

The first issue, for example, featured a defense of hipsters, which pushed back on the mockery they had engendered online, especially in a *Salon* piece that reported on hipsters applying for food stamps. The piece, by the author Peter Frase, argued that public goods and benefits should be widely shared and easily accessible, and if a recent college graduate went on food stamps so that they could pursue their art or their music or just live their life as they saw fit, the should feel free to do so.

But Sunkara and the magazine as a whole argued for the Left to reconfigure its way of thinking. The Left had been too content to march through the streets in black sweatshirts or sleep out in Zuccotti Park or encourage consumer boycotts, but it had been afraid to organize itself into a rational structure and especially afraid to take power.

"The Left wants to change the world without taking power," Sunkara observed. "They are comfortable with being fringe." But, he asserted, "we think these ideas, about greater democracy in our politics, greater democracy in the workplace, paid family leave, Medicare for All, paid childcare, are very popular and that we should talk about them and try to enact them."

The magazine scarcely wrote about AOC during her race, but she sat for interviews after she won and was quoted in articles by other interviewers. And in many ways, she embodies the *Jacobin* project, a politically engaged leftism that is building political power and that comes from the working class, and that pays attention to the aesthetic styles of the moment and tries to engage with the wider culture at large.

Sunkara considered AOC to be "an incredible advocate for broadly social democratic ideas," finding it "significant that she was a bartender until two years ago. The promise of our work is maybe not every cook in a restaurant kitchen could participate in organizing their workplace and or political engagement, but probably most of them can."

It is likely that Alexandria Ocasio-Cortez's campaign would have languished in obscurity had not Matt Stoller, an author, an economic historian, and a fellow at Open Markets Institute in New York, caught wind of her bid in late 2017. He texted his friend Ryan Grim, a longtime Washington reporter who had recently taken a job as the DC bureau chief at *The Intercept*, "Hey do you know anything about Alexandria Ocasio-Cortez and her challenge to Crowley in Queens?"

Grim didn't know anything but looked into the campaign finance report and found it substantial (only later realizing that, in fact, he had misread the report, and Ocasio-Cortez had a fraction of the money on hand he had thought). Grim, figuring it would be a good chance to introduce Crowley to a national audience—since he was likely the next Speaker of the House anyway—sent a reporter and a photographer to cover Ocasio-Cortez. In May 2018, he cowrote *The Intercept*'s first story on the long-shot candidate titled "A Primary Against the Machine: A Bronx Activist Looks to Dethrone Joseph Crowley, the King of Queens."[4]

The piece introduced readers to Ocasio-Cortez, running through the highlights of her biography—the move to Westchester for a better education, her father's sudden passing, the years spent keeping lawyers at bay from foreclosure—but it was mostly a withering rundown of the ways in which Crowley had grown out of touch with a district and a county he was supposed to rule over like a rajah.

It described Crowley as someone in hock to Wall Street financial interests, more interested in the Dow Jones Industrial Average than in the economic futures of his largely working-class constituents in the outer boroughs. The story painted Crowley as someone whose prolific fundraising for the Democratic Congressional Campaign Committee meant that he was on the cusp of becoming the next Speaker of the House, and as someone who was consolidating his power in Queens County, which would grant him unprecedented home and away power for a sitting member of Congress.

Subtle, in other words, the piece wasn't. It talked about Crowley shifting his fundraising from unions to financial services. The article also mentioned that he had been investigated by the House Ethics Committee and that he freely gave out his largesse to "moderate and conservative Democratic candidates around the country"—never mind the money he doled out to progressives. His tenure atop the head of the Queens County Democratic Party—an organization that, as we were all soon to learn, was so hollowed out that it couldn't protect its leader against a twenty-eight-year-old bartender—gave Crowley "power throughout the borough in a number of overlapping and interlocking ways," which he used to handpick judges and candidates and keep disfavored would-be candidates off the ballot.[5]

"Crowley's power—both locally and nationally—could theoretically be used for the benefit of the people of the district," the story continued. "In reality, though, Ocasio-Cortez said he's used it to benefit Wall Street and luxury real-estate developers, who are gentrifying the district and pushing working-class people out."[6]

That article was just the first of a dozen that tracked the Ocasio-Cortez/Crowley race, a race that went largely unnoticed by the rest of the national press and even by much of the local press, save for a few articles in hyperlocal news outlets. The *New York Times* only mentioned Ocasio-Cortez once in a story about a new wave of female candidates and another time in an editorial chastising Crowley for skipping a scheduled debate with her.

But *The Intercept* more than took up the slack. Having recognized a good story, it went all in, covering the twists and turns of the campaign in a way it hadn't for any other race before.

Crowley's campaign team started to seethe, believing that by the end of the race the site was little more than an in-kind contribution to the Ocasio-Cortez for Congress campaign. "Joe Crowley Complains His Primary Opponent Alexandria Ocasio-Cortez Is Making This Race 'About Race'" screamed one headline. The story went on to quote someone who heard the candidate tell a crowd at a backyard fundraiser that Ocasio-Cortez was running a racially divisive campaign and that, "I can't help that I was born white."[7]

The piece went on to detail how Crowley, whose uncle served as a city councilor, got the job in Congress: when Congressman Tom Manton was ready to retire, he handpicked Crowley as his replacement at the last possible minute in order to fend off any primary challenges. The article gave lots of room for Alexandria Ocasio-Cortez to make the anti-Crowley case.

"The irony that Crowley laments how he 'can't help' being white, while ignoring the political advantages he inherited, is not lost on Ocasio-Cortez," wrote Grim, who proceeded to quote Ocasio-Cortez:

> The congressman could have helped that he accepted inheritance of his seat from a multigenerational political dynasty without a true primary—a process by which people of color are historically locked out of representation. The congressman could help that he voted to establish ICE. The congressman can help the fact that he accepts money from developers that are displacing our communities and the folks criminalizing our backyards. Additionally, why is it that the congressman can proudly discuss his Irish heritage on the campaign trail, but I am somehow barred from mentioning my Puerto Rican family?[8]

As Grim saw it, AOC was what the left wing of the party was looking for after Bernie Sanders's failed 2016 run.

"We knew this needed to be a multiracial movement after 2016," Grim told me. "An older white guy has a harder time winning Black voters, and that is something the establishment uses to beat back insurgent candidates. I knew this district needed an outsider, a Latina, a working-class woman candidate. People were called racist and sexist in 2016 for supporting Sanders, and Ocasio-Cortez was able to precisely articulate what is meant by class intersectionality. You can't understand how exciting that was for people on the Left."[9]

There were other stories too—a video interview with Glenn Greenwald, the founding editor of *The Intercept*, in which AOC accused Crowley of being funded by the very same donors who supported Donald Trump. "My opponent takes an insane amount of money from luxury real-estate developers, from private equity groups, from pharmaceutical corporations, and private insurance corporations," AOC noted. "And that is tied directly to the legislation that he's been passing. And you look at, for example, you know, eight or seven of his top ten donors are primarily Republican financers, his number two top donor is [the private equity firm] Blackstone.

They primarily financed the Trump presidency."[10] Ocasio-Cortez received other press coverage: a story about how Crowley's tenure as head of the Queens County Democratic Party had enriched some of his allies,[11] another about how AOC scored the endorsement of the lefty outfit MoveOn.org,[12] another about the socialist ad makers who produced her viral campaign ad,[13] another that reported on her lone televised debate with Crowley,[14] another about how identity politics were complicating the narratives of the race,[15] and a handful of others.

On the night that AOC won the race, *The Intercept* was the only media outlet at her victory party; other local outlets tried to get in when it became clear that Ocasio-Cortez could win, but her staff, smarting about the lack of coverage of the race, refused to let any enter.

"We're rabble rousers," said Grim, the author of several of those AOC stories, referring to *The Intercept*. "I have been covering the Capitol for twelve years, and my work is better because I have really good access to the most powerful people in Washington. We were pretty sure she was going to lose, but we figured it was an interesting and compelling story, and I knew that by going all in on it we would be burning all of those networks to the ground."

Grim joined *The Intercept* in June 2017. Prior to his arrival, the outlet was mostly known for its scorching coverage of the national security state in a post-9/11 world, particularly the National Security Agency's drone strike assassination program and its plan to increase its surveillance net around the world. Much of the information came from Edward Snowden, the former CIA contractor who revealed previously unknown details of the government's spying program.

The Intercept—founded by Greenwald and two other editors and funded by Pierre Omidyar, the billionaire founder of eBay—was created in part to provide a platform for Snowden, to encourage more of the same from similarly placed sources, and to provide editorial independence and protection for the journalists who write about national security issues.

The founders planned to write about other issues in a similar vein: criminal justice, inequality, corruption, and the media. "The editorial independence of our journalists will be guaranteed, and they will be encouraged to pursue their journalistic passion, areas of interest, and unique voices," the editors wrote in their opening memo. "We believe the prime value of journalism is that it imposes transparency, and thus accountability, on those who wield the greatest governmental and corporate power. Our journalists will be not only permitted, but encouraged, to pursue stories without re-gard to whom they might alienate."[16]

"Our tagline is 'fearless, adversarial journalism,' and that kind of sums up our approach," executive editor Betsy Reed told me in her office overlooking lower Fifth Avenue in Manhattan. "It's an outsider approach. There is the kind of coverage that lends itself to a kind of access journalism, and then there is what we do which cultivates whistle-blowers as sources."

Reed came to The Intercept from The Nation, where she had served as executive editor for nine years, hoping to do a different kind of journalism than the one at that august institution of left politics, one that focused more on money in politics and took more of an adversarial approach to the Democratic Party.

The Intercept's political coverage became supercharged when Reed hired Grim. He had spent several years as the DC bureau chief at the Huffington Post. He was thought to be the next editor in chief of the site after founder Arianna Huffington stepped down, but when the job went instead to New York Times correspondent Lydia Polgreen, he left the company. Grim had been one of the original hires at Politico, and he grew into one of the site's star reporters on Capitol Hill. He was concerned that when he left the nonpartisan Politico for the left-leaning Huffington Post, it would mean he had lost access to his sources in the GOP leadership, but Grim told me that a senior House Republican aide reassured him that it would be fine, saying, "We always knew you were a communist, Grim."

Grim's parents divorced when he was young, and he grew up on the rural Eastern Shore of Maryland on food stamps and free school lunches while his mom worked a series of low-wage jobs. His father was a school counselor in Allentown, Pennsylvania, and lived relatively comfortably. Grim traveled between the two worlds every other weekend, which gave him a sense of the randomness and unfairness of the economic divide. He was at graduate school at the University of Maryland, studying for a degree in public policy, when he took a journalism class with Gene Roberts, the legendary editor at the *Philadelphia Inquirer*. As a student, Grim wrote a piece on the sudden scarcity of LSD, which got picked up by *Slate*. After graduation, he got a job at a brokerage firm, hoping to serve as an undercover journalist who would then write a tell-all piece about the rot inside American capitalism. "Confessions of an Outlaw Stock Jockey" was published in the anarchist-inflected *Brooklyn Rail* in 2002, but it didn't have the seismic impact Grim had hoped for, and he soon moved to Washington to become a lobbyist for the Marijuana Policy Project but later drifted into journalism.

From his perch at *The Intercept*, Grim has made the site into a champion of outsider candidates, taking aim at what it viewed as the corrupt class of DC insiders. The site has, for example, published leaked audio of Steny Hoyer, the second-highest-ranking Democrat in the House, trying to dissuade an outsider candidate from running, and a "groggy-voiced recording" of Gil Cisneros, a party-backed congressional candidate in California, left on the voicemail of the wife of one of his insurgent opponents, warning that he was about to go negative. Neither of these stories was particularly scandalous or outside the bounds of politics—congressional leaders are allowed to go pick favorites, and no rules prohibit candidates from calling one another—but *The Intercept* played them as the machinations of a Machiavellian political machine.

"The problem with the Democratic Party is that too many people are dying because they lack healthcare, too many people are being run through the school-to-prison pipeline, too many people are seeing their future destroyed by going to shitty public schools, too many people are in poverty, and too many Democratic leaders are comfortable with the status quo," Grim said. "They think maybe things can be made a bit better, but there is no sense of urgency. So we have one side, the Republicans, who are against progress, and another side, the Democrats who think it isn't worth it to fight for it, that it will go nowhere. And somebody needs to fight for it."

Both Reed and Grim say *The Intercept* provides a necessary correction among a news media that has its own unrecognized biases against the status quo.

"I think that for a lot of journalists, they think of someone like Joe Crowley, 'Oh, he is a part of our world.' And they are not going to bring scrutiny to him," Reed said. "But every utterance that someone like Ilhan Omar makes gets blown up and catches fire because that is the mentality of most media professionals."

Reed compared the way most news outlets cover politics to the way most news outlets cover war: they embed someone on the frontlines, and that reporter develops relationships with soldiers and military brass. At *The Nation*, Reed published reports by Ann Jones, a journalist who embedded with Afghani women's groups during the American war in Afghanistan, so that readers got a view of what women on the ground were going through.

"Our reporters have to understand that they are players in the political system, not mere observers. They should never push their coverage in a particular direction to achieve a particular outcome, but they have to understand that journalism has consequences," said Grim. He pointed to Hunter Thompson's famous 1975 *Rolling Stone* profile of Jimmy Carter, which gave the obscure Georgia governor a boost that helped launch him into the White House.

"All journalists want to have an impact. That means that somebody wins and somebody loses. The *New York Times* is whipsawing around this [2020 Democratic primary] campaign, first giving one candidate a boost, then another, deflating one, then another. We just recognize what we are doing," Grim said.[17]

Advocacy journalism has a long and storied lineage in American journalism. It is journalism that announces its bias upfront and that proudly pushes for a cause, counting Nellie Bly, Lincoln Steffens, and probably half the investigative reporters in America among its ranks. But what *The Intercept* does is different. Advocacy journalism means advocating for specific issues and causes. Reed, Grim, Greenwald, and their staff advocate for—or at least come very close to advocating for—specific candidates in political races. The Crowley's staff charge that *The Intercept's* coverage amounted to little more than an in-kind gift to AOC's campaign wasn't wrong.

"We see it as our jobs to give oxygen and attention to candidates who are critics of the way politics generally operates," said Reed. "We make clear the things we are committed to, like civil rights and privacy, human rights for immigrants. We have a set of values and we don't insist that reporters hide who they are. And so when we write a story about a candidate who wants to abolish ICE, the story is going to be sympathetic to that goal."

Grim agrees. During the 2020 campaign, Bernie Sanders was briefly off the trail after suffering a heart attack and returned with a mega rally in Queens with AOC and twenty thousand supporters. Backstage, the duo granted interviews to a couple of television networks and to Grim and *The Intercept* team, who uploaded it to their YouTube channel.

"It is in some sense new territory, yes," Grim said. "When I was at the *Huffington Post*, we had good relationships with Nancy Pelosi, Harry Reid, Elizabeth Warren, people like that, and it is something you constantly need to think about in your reporting and writing. But on the other hand, you don't want to be a nihilist who is attacking power for the sake of attacking power. That is not useful either. We have to hold AOC to account. But if she is doing what she said she was going to do, I don't see any reason to drag her."

Emma Vigeland discovered *The Young Turks* when she was still in middle school in Montclair, New Jersey. It was the 2008 Democratic primary between Hillary Clinton and Barack Obama, and CNN and the rest of the news networks seemed to her all in on Clinton.

"I thought, I really like this Obama guy, so like a true millennial I went looking for him on YouTube," she said. "And I found this really angry guy who kept on screaming about the Bush administration."

She was head of her high school's Young Democrats club and used to try to show the club these strange videos during meetings, but the club's adviser eventually forbade them as "too fiery."

That angry guy was Cenk Uygur, someone who bounced around in the liberal mediasphere at places like MSNBC and the defunct Current TV, before finding success as the founder and face of *The Young Turks*, a progressive news and commentary program that is the flagship show on a network of the same name.

If *The Intercept* has become the publishing outlet of choice for the resistance inside the Democratic Party, the Young Turks is their broadcast counterpart. It is a television network that does not broadcast on television but instead operates a 24-7 YouTube channel out of a 5,200-square-foot studio on Wilshire Boulevard in central Los Angeles. That channel gets 250 million monthly views and has 4.1 million subscribers, and its videos have more than 4 billion views. After Trump's election, the network received $20 million in venture capital funding from a group that included Hollywood producer and former Walt Disney chairman Jeffrey Katzenberg.[18] It has more viewers under twenty-five online than CNN, Fox News, and MSNBC combined.

Vigeland got an internship at the network in 2016, just after finishing college, figuring it would be something for her to do in the year before applying to law school. She had no experience in politics or journalism or television but started working behind the scenes, helping with production, studying what made for good TV and what didn't. A year later, one of *The Young Turks'* main correspondents, Jordan Chariton, was fired after allegations of sexual misconduct surfaced, and Vigeland took over his spot.

She began taking the lead on the politics coverage and soon learned about Ocasio-Cortez's candidacy.

And if *The Intercept* was the first print outlet to go deep on Ocasio-Cortez and her race, they were late-comers to the party compared to *The Young Turks*. In the winter of 2018, Vigeland knocked on the door of Ocasio-Cortez's Bronx apartment—the one with the Bernie 2016 sticker on it—and entered a small, tidy apartment with modern art on the walls and a lone campaign staffer.

Inside, AOC laid out her case to Vigeland: how she was born in Parkchester, grew up upstate to get a better education, had organized for Bernie, and had traveled to Flint, Michigan, and Standing Rock. "New York City politics is a crazy place to be, and I never really envisioned myself here," she told Vigeland. "I really feel like we are at a point in our democracy where we need to be firing on all cylinders. And we need to be challenging the establishment everywhere that it is. And this is my place in that broader revolution."

The two ended up spending eight hours together, mostly walking side by side around the neighborhood or on AOC's long bus commute from the Bronx into Queens or sitting in a local restaurant.

It wasn't so much an interview as a conversation between two people, interrupting and bouncing ideas off each other. They talked about how unlivable and expensive New York was, how homeownership was an impossibility—something they blamed on corrupt politicians more than simple supply and demand—how Uber was pushing out Yellow Cab drivers, and how the Democratic Party had been allowed to rot from the inside.

They talked public policy too, in a way that most long-shot congressional candidates don't get asked about, mostly because it is so hard to have an impact from the back bench. Yet Ocasio-Cortez called for free public colleges, for good union jobs like the ones that were provided for the grounds crew in the housing complex where she lived, and for a massive public investment in switching to a green economy.

"We have to invest in changing to a renewable energy economy in fifteen years. Some people say twenty, fifty [years], but we actually think that when we look at these numbers, we see that it's possible on a shorter timeline. And in order for our generation to survive life as we know it and maintain a sense of normalcy, we need to switch to renewable energy as quickly as possible," AOC said.

AOC noted that often those on the right, and some in the center, charge that renewable energy and creating jobs aren't economically viable, but she asserted that "those are always the same people taking the money from the industries where they're incentivized to say that. So it sounded [like it was] about economic growth. When you hear that talking point, it's really about preserving the already existing power structures. . . . And when people talk about things not being economically viable, they're thinking about short-term returns. They're not thinking about the long-term economy." AOC observed that businesses and special interests focus on "what's going to give me a profit in Q1 or Q2, which often are these Band-Aid solutions. But it's our job as citizens and members of government to think about the long-term and to think about how we're not only gonna survive but thrive seven generations on."

They spoke about what it was like to be a Democrat in New York and to run as an outsider in a city and state that may be one of the most liberal in the nation, which ensures its political class is kept cosseted from any kind of political challenges. At the time, New York's governor Andrew Cuomo, a figure hated by much of the Left for governing from the center in a deep blue state, was facing a primary challenge by Cynthia Nixon, the former star of *Sex and the City*, and Vigeland asked AOC what she thought of the race. She didn't answer directly—Nixon didn't endorse AOC until the race's waning days—but used the opportunity to talk about the daunting political hurdles she was forced to overcome as an outsider candidate.

"I think one of the big things that we have to face as New Yorkers is that a lot of our voting issues are less about the stance and more about the execution," she said. "And I think we really need to have a real conversation about corruption in the city. We need to have a conversation about corruption in the state because everyone runs as a Democrat. There is so much corruption that we tolerate it just because a person puts a D in front of their name and it's my opinion that we need to hold our elected officials more accountable for what's going on."

After the interview, Vigeland called her mother in New Jersey and said that she had just spent the afternoon with a political star.

"She was extremely warm, and, politically, she was just speaking my language," recalled Vigeland. "It's the language of grassroots progressive politics that I had been waiting for someone to talk about."

The Young Turks is a different kind of journalism from what we are used to seeing on cable news, one that is unapologetic about its political biases and its efforts to boost chosen candidates and give them a platform.

"My entire goal is to change the world for the better," Vigeland said. "That's what drives me, as opposed to being a newsperson. Although it is fun to go on cable and get your makeup done and stuff like that, but I'd give all of that up to change the country."

The AOC campaign and victory was a big moment for *The Young Turks* as well. Vigeland's interview with AOC, which spanned several segments, was one of thirty-four times that candidate Ocasio-Cortez appeared on *The Young Turks*, which was thirty-four more times than she appeared on any other television broadcast. Uygur was one of the founding members of Justice Democrats but had been forced to step down when a series of misogynistic blog posts he had written in the early 2000s was unearthed. ("It seems like there is a sea of tits here, and I am drinking in tiny droplets. I want to dive into the whole god damn ocean," he wrote in one. "Obviously, the genes of women are flawed. They are poorly designed creatures who do not want to have sex nearly as often as needed for the human race to get along peaceably and fruitfully.")[19]

But Uygur remained invested in the project and early on saw AOC as the best hope for success among Justice Democrat-endorsed candidates..

One of the excuses Uygur gave for the blog posts was that he wrote them when he was still a Republican. It is true that Uygur did first rise to prominence as a Republican, writing in campus newspapers as an undergraduate and later as a law student. He joined the Federalist Society, railed against left-wing bias on campus, got a public access television show, and tried to make it as a right-wing talk radio shock jock, even interviewing to be a replacement for Fox News's Sean Hannity at one point.

It is not much of an excuse, nor is it an accurate one. In 2019, Uygur announced that he was running for Congress himself, and a spate of stories of Uygur denigrating women and minorities re-emerged, leading Bernie Sanders and other progressives to distance themselves from him; among those stories were incidents on his show where Uygur ranked women and described them in crude and sexualized terms, defended misogynistic acts by other men, and used a number of racial and religious slurs. He lost the race.[20]

The impeachment of Bill Clinton, the soaring deficits of the Bush era, and the Iraq War turned Uygur into a liberal. He started a Sirius radio show with Ben Mankiewicz, now a host of Turner Classic Movies, and called it *The Young Turks*, since the hosts fashioned themselves as young progressives attempting to overthrow the establishment. Times were serious, and they became leading public critics of the Iraq War at a time when much of the media was not, which taught Uygur another lesson: "we are right and they are wrong."

"The media never stops being wrong," he said. "No matter how many times they've been wrong before. And they keep saying we're the crazy ones, even though we've been proven correct almost every single time. The media says we are a center-right country. And they say that because they are biased. They're economically conservative. They live in a bubble; they love the status quo. The rest of the country hates the status quo." Uygur asserted, "We're progressives, and on issue after issue, so is the country. We're populists, and we're outsiders, and that's where ninety-eight percent of the country is. The problem is that there is the two percent that is elitist, that loves the status quo, and they are in charge."

Uygur eventually got the idea to film the radio show—bringing on guests from the mainstream media like Dana Milbank of the *Washington Post* and Michael Isikoff of *Newsweek*—and then posting it on their website or on YouTube. Progressive politics were so hard to find on TV—even MSNBC hadn't pivoted fully to the left—that the show gathered a small but loyal audience.

As Uygur sees it, *The Young Turks* provides "factual correctness," while the rest of the media is focused on "political correctness"—that is, playing both sides of every issue in a way that advantages Republicans. "Our role is to make the world more equitable, to make progressive politics more prominent in this country and give a voice to the powerless and underdog candidates in this country in order to achieve Medicare for All and a Green New Deal and all the other things that we care about."

Throughout its history, *The Young Turks* has grown by relying on its cohort of devoted viewers. Uygur has bounced around from MSNBC—where he was given a weekend time slot he ultimately lost because, according to network head Phil Griffin, Uygur's "feisty attitude" made it hard to book guests—to Current TV, which soon went off the air, while always keeping the radio show and its attendant web broadcast going. At one point, Uygur asked his audience for $125,000 so that they could expand their studio, and they raised $425,000. After Trump's election, he asked for money to hire an investigative reporting team, and *The Young Turks* audience donated $2 million for the effort.

"Our audience loves us, because we are the only ones that represent them," Uygur said. "We're progressive and we're loud and we're unapologetic and no one else is."

CHAPTER 7

THE GREEN NEW WORLD

People dismayed at the election of Donald Trump reacted in all sorts of ways. Some took to the streets. Some organized in their local communities. Some retreated into despair.

Alexandria Ocasio-Cortez drove with two friends to a Native American reservation in North Dakota.

Protests at the Standing Rock Reservation began in March 2016, when nearly two hundred members of several Lakota Sioux tribes gathered at the Tribal Administration Building and rode on horseback twenty-five miles north to the town of Cannonball, North Dakota, on the northern edge of the reservation. They were there to protest the Dakota Access Pipeline, a 1,172-mile pipeline that carried crude oil across the Dakotas to Illinois. New developments in hydrofracking technology had opened up the Bakken oil field to drilling, and supporters of the pipeline said the project would create jobs and help wean the nation off of foreign oil. Opponents said that building more pipelines would only keep the nation from dealing with an overreliance on fossil fuels and contribute further to catastrophic climate change. But the members of the Native American tribes who showed up to protest had more immediate concerns: the pipeline would travel beneath the Missouri River, an important water source for the Standing Rock Sioux tribe, and it would cross over some of the tribe's sacred burial grounds.

"This is sacred land," LaDonna Allard, a member of the Standing Rock Sioux tribe told Britain's *Guardian* newspaper, which covered the uprising far more closely than any American paper. "This is not about trying to be a protester. I am a mother. My son is buried at the top of that hill. I can't let them build a pipeline by my son's grave."[1]

In August 2016, hundreds of protesters from around the country gathered at the tribe's encampment, jumping fences and surrounding construction machinery. A few days later, the workers returned, accompanied by armed guards, and the number of protesters grew, too, numbering between four hundred and five hundred with another few hundred camping nearby on either side of the Cannonball River.

That camp was more than just a place to stay. It became a gathering point, not just for rival tribes but for people from all over. It began to resemble the parking lot of a rock concert crossed with a tribal gathering—there were sweat lodges and teepees, tents and portable toilets, and stands selling food and hand-crafted art. Throughout the camp, protesters participated in prayer groups, rituals, and ceremonies, and tribal members rode horses for sport and to patrol the grounds. At the camp's center was a firepit, where protesters gathered to pray, bang drums, plan actions, and stage ceremonial dances.

As the 2016 presidential election approached, the population of the encampment swelled even further, and clashes among the protesters and police grew more violent. Bernie Sanders, CNN analyst Van Jones, and actor Shailene Woodley joined the protest, and journalists like *Democracy Now* host Amy Goodman were nearly arrested for reporting on the conflict. On the last Friday of October, police fired beanbag rounds and pepper spray at protesters and arrested 142 people. Two days later, millions attended a virtual protest on Facebook, where users "checked in" at Standing Rock in order to confuse police surveillance.

Just before the election, Obama floated the notion that the pipeline could be moved off of the contested grounds, and after Trump won, but before he had taken office, Obama called for a more thorough environmental review of the project. Trump scuttled that plan almost immediately after being sworn in, and the protests flared up again, only to die out as the last parts of the project were completed.

Before protesters started amassing in North Dakota, there was another localized environmental and public health issue that was attracting the world's attention. Flint, Michigan, was once an automobile manufacturing mecca, home to a sprawling network of eight General Motors plants, where, in the 1930s, 136,000 workers walked off the job to demand better working conditions, an action that helped spur the creation of the United Auto Workers labor union.

In the years since, however, the plants moved out to the suburbs and then closed completely, and the city's workforce and population shrank. In 2014, the city, bankrupt and crime-ridden, ended its relationship with Detroit Water and Sewerage Department for water supply, building instead its own pipeline with the Karegnondi Water Authority in an effort to save money. To keep water flowing in the meantime, the city tapped into the Flint River as its main water source, as the city had in the 1960s.

Almost immediately, residents knew something was wrong. The water smelled off and tasted wrong, too, even though officials insisted the water was safe to drink and bathe in. Thousands of children ended up with elevated levels of lead in their bloodstream, a condition that can stunt physical and mental growth. Dozens are believed to have died from a Legionnaires' disease outbreak tied to the unsafe water conditions.

The story of Flint and its water shocked the nation. Hillary Clinton called it "unconscionable" in the 2016 campaign, and Bernie Sanders, at a campaign event in early 2016, called the whole episode "painful" and "horrific." "What country am I living in? Is this the United States of America?" he asked the crowd at a campaign rally in Michigan. "I fear that Flint is the canary in the coal mine here."

After Trump's shocking win that November, Ocasio-Cortez found herself adrift. "My family wasn't a labor family, a union family," she told me. "My mom scrubbed toilets, that's who we were. And then after [organizing for Bernie Sanders] and then after November I felt I couldn't go back to doing nothing anymore and that my space was activism. And that's when I went to South Dakota and I just started saying, 'I'm just going to show up. The best thing I can do is show up.'"

The night after the presidential election, Ocasio-Cortez wrote her thoughts about what had just occurred on Facebook.

Social instability is a direct result of wealth inequality. And bigotry is a [sic] largely a result of poverty and scarcity. I know this may be hard to believe, but take refuge in the fact that sexism, racism, and xenophobia did not win last night. They were attendants to a larger stage. What won was the fight for struggling, working class people to be heard. And although I did not wish (nor vote) for this outcome, I at least seek to understand it.

Like it or not, you will have to listen to the clear message working Americans sent last night. Do your part to fight for higher wages. Question and examine the TPP [Trans-Pacific Partnership] (which, despite enormous public sentiment to the contrary, Obama is still seeking to pass). Care about who is funding your candidates and why. Hold them accountable for their transparency or lack thereof. Take poverty and economic despair seriously. This is an opportunity to dig deeper in your compassion for others—because in truly loving your so-called enemies (and not ignoring them), you can transform them and yourself for the better. By ignoring them, you run the risk of tyranny committed by either them or yourself.

If you truly love others, you will go beyond the fight against racism—for that is an effort to change a man's attitude. By fighting for economic justice, you seek to change his life. This is the path forward.[2]

A few weeks later, just a week before Christmas, Ocasio-Cortez set sail on a road trip that would take her both to Flint and to

Standing Rock, traveling with two friends from New York, Maria Swisher and Joshua Pereira, and raising money online for supplies for Standing Rock protesters.

"After the events of this year, my good friend Maria Swisher and I began to feel the strain of feeling disconnected from people of different backgrounds, opinions, politics, etc.," AOC wrote on social media. "We feel that the tenor of our national discourse has worn down to an extent that people everywhere were having a difficult time finding common ground and talking honestly. We wanted to do something about it."

Driving in a borrowed '98 Subaru station wagon, the three friends drove to Cleveland, arriving at three o'clock in the morning, and set off just a few hours later for Flint. "I just don't know how something like this happens and we don't have pressure on leadership in the state of Michigan," Ocasio-Cortez said on one of the many Facebook livestreams the group produced. "It's so concerning that someone could keep their job and really fail the essential structure of government—keeping people safe. And not in an accidental way, but in a negligent way. Flint is just the tip of the iceberg. There are countless other cities . . . that have contaminated drinking water and they just don't know it."

In Flint the group had lunch with Frank Woods, then the executive director of the Flint Housing Commission, a low-income housing agency in the city. Woods told them what living in Flint was like at that moment, after much of the media caravan, which had come to town a year or two before, had left. He told them that residents were paying for water they couldn't use and that too many people were focused on what had gone wrong instead of what needed to happen. People in Flint were still engaged in the political process, said Woods, but their patience was running out, and they were tiring of politicians coming to town for photo ops and with promises to fix the problem. AOC asked if people still voted, and Woods said they did.

"To me, after everything that happened here, after governments essentially poisoned their children's water, created neurological deficits and there are very few resources and they are trying to cobble together solutions, the fact that they are still going to city council meetings is just incredible to me," AOC said.

Woods was a veteran, a former charter school assistant principal, a pastor, and the founder of a nonprofit organization to serve the homeless before becoming head of the Flint Housing Commission. He told the group that his first love was politics but that politics didn't love him back, a comment that struck a chord with AOC.

"This is the problem, these really talented and passionate and community-minded people can't be politicians, and that is something that is really wrong with our system," said Swisher, an actor and a friend of Ocasio-Cortez from their bartending days. AOC nodded along on their livestream. "It takes so much money, and frankly corruption, to be a politician."

You could almost see the wheels turning in AOC's mind as the two continued on from their drive from Flint.

"I was really asking a lot of questions, trying to figure out where did this breakdown happen?" AOC said. "Where did it start? Was it our local politicians bought out? Is it the state? Is it a bureaucratic thing? Is there a private corporation here? Is it that people don't care and are not paying attention to what's going on? And it seems as though when you connect some of these disparate thoughts, it all does come back down to the influence of money in politics."

Just twenty-seven years old, Ocasio-Cortez was wrestling with the notion that protest could be of limited value, that it might be more important to actually engage in politics and government.

"I think that while protest can be effective in certain contexts, it is not a panacea," she concluded. "We just saw an intense amount of public spotlight thrust upon Flint, which is the aim of protest, to create a spotlight on the situation. In Flint, they just experienced that spotlight and nothing happened."

Ocasio-Cortez brooded on these questions as she and her friends made their way west. The issue of the pipeline was complicated, she said, but what wasn't was the issue of sovereignty. New York had banned fracking, and so it ceased to exist in the state; the people of the Standing Rock didn't want a pipeline running through their land, and so they deserved to be heard and to have their say as well.

"It goes back to this fundamental value. We are one. We are one nation and what happens to some of us happens to all of us," she said on one livestream. "When children's water are [sic] being contaminated in Flint, it's my business. When people's lives are in danger because their sovereignty is at risk, in my country, it is my business. A threat to you is a threat to me. And to close my eyes in the face of my neighbor's injustice opens the door to my injustice."[3]

The group arrived at Standing Rock on a bright and fiercely cold, windswept night on December 21, the longest night of the year. They were stopped by armed guards in green fatigues who directed them to drive farther south and enter the reservation from the South Dakota side. The group entered the camp at night the next day, traveling down a road flanked with the flags of the various tribes, passing a massive bonfire and someone playing the flute. There were more stars lighting up the night than AOC had ever seen.

The next morning, AOC, her friends, and the rest of the two thousand or so people gathered by the ceremonial fire pit for predawn prayers. At sunrise, they chanted, "Mní wičóni," a Lakota phrase meaning "water is life."

While at Standing Rock, they slept in a tent warmed by a wood-burning stove, interviewed some of the protesters, went to camp meetings, and returned back to New York with a newly restored faith in humanity and a determination to spread what they learned there far and wide.

AOC and her friends had come to Standing Rock in the hopes of delivering supplies to a group of protesters who were out in the Dakota winter. When they arrived, they were surprised not just to find a tent waiting for them but people asking them if they needed anything. Someone gave them warm socks because the ones they had were inadequate, and they passed the pair on when they left. When supplies arrived, people took only what they needed and left the rest for others. When trash was on the ground, it got picked up. When disputes came up, mostly over tactics, they got sorted out peaceably through mediation. They stopped by the sacred fire on their way out, and two camp elders asked if there was a prayer they could say for them.

People who knew Ocasio-Cortez, friends from college and high school, took notice of this trip, aware that she planned and carefully documented it on social media, where she garnered a decent-sized audience for someone whose celebrity didn't extend much beyond the restaurant where she worked. They noticed that she seemed to be stepping out on her own, expanding her world since it had constricted after the death of her father.

Before they left the camp, the three friends went live in another Facebook post, and Ocasio-Cortez recounted something an elder, a Native veteran, had told her at the camp, that "who you are right now and where you are right now is intrinsically tied to and a reflection of the actions of people seven generations past and that your decisions will echo seven generations into the future." And by this telling the United States, in 2016, was precisely seven generations removed from its founding. "This generation, if you are alive, if you are present, if you are awake in America right now, you are a very important person. You're at a very important inflection point in this country and what we choose now is going to change the next seven generations in the future."

"The elders of the camp," she continued, "truly believe that young people will change the world. That this generation of young people will change the world, that we are at the inflection point of seven generations, since America's founding and we are now about to embark on seven generations into America's future. They really feel like people are starting to wake up."

Julian Brave NoiseCat was going to go to Standing Rock in the winter of 2016, too, but leaders of the protest asked him to stay away. By early winter, there were already upward of two thousand people camping on-site, and more people would only put more pressure on the leaders to keep everyone safe, warm, and well fed.

Raised by a single mother in Oakland, NoiseCat, a member of the Secwépemc tribe, spent his childhood in the East Bay and among the Secwépemc and St'at'imc territories in British Columbia, Canada. There, he learned how to dipnet and dry salmon and traveled on the powwow circuit, while back home in Oakland he became steeped in the American Indian Movement and the civil rights movement, both of which were nurtured decades before there.[4]

NoiseCat ended up at Columbia University in New York and then studied at Oxford, but returned to New York after watching the Bernie Sanders campaign flare up and flame out from afar and deciding that he wanted to be closer to the action.

And so he got a civil servant job with the city of New York and started organizing local actions around the Standing Rock pipeline, once getting arrested in front of the Army Corps of Engineers building in Lower Manhattan in a traffic-stopping protest. He also hosted teach-ins, wrote articles, and gave talks about how the battle over Standing Rock was the catalyst for both a new kind of resistance from Native Americans and the dawn of a new era of environmental activism.

"It showed for the first time in modern American history that indigenous people could lead a movement that mattered to a broader public instead of just our own," NoiseCat said in an interview. "That messages about climate change and water and environmental justice could matter to a community larger than our own when the whole country was focused on Donald Trump. It was really the closing of one chapter of the environmental movement and the opening of another."

The Standing Rock protest was in many ways the continuation of a series of protests that had begun in previous years. Those protests were also centered on stopping pipelines and other energy infrastructures, most notably the Keystone Pipeline, which was slated to run through the Upper Midwest but not across native lands and which was ultimately killed by Barack Obama (although brought back to life by Donald Trump in his first days in office). In states around the country, protesters had been catalyzed by the prospect of new pipelines running through their communities, and in many cases, the opposition was enough to defeat the project.

The Keystone protests had been catalyzed by Bill McKibben, an activist, an author, and one of the founders of 350.org, an environmental organization named for the 350 parts per million of carbon dioxide in the atmosphere, which would signify a climatological tipping point. The group led an International Day of Climate Action in 2010, which was the largest global demonstration in a single day in support of mitigation efforts to combat global warming. The event included climate marches in cities around the world and helped spur student-led efforts on US college campuses to force schools to divest from fossil fuel companies.

Those efforts had been the focus of much of the climate movement during the Obama years, but after Trump was elected, environmental activists came to believe that something new and more dramatic was needed. They wanted to get beyond just stopping infrastructure projects, to be *for* something rather than just *against* things.

The Bernie Sanders campaign in 2015 and 2016 had shown there was an appetite for maximalist policy ideas that would have been unthinkable for a national candidate even a few years earlier. Medicare for All and free college hadn't been discussed in previous years, not even by candidates proclaiming to represent the progressive wing of the Democratic Party, and here more than 40 percent of the party's primary voters were rallying behind those issues.

Sanders's climate proposals were slightly less ambitious, however, than some of his economic ones. He called for banning fossil fuel lobbyists from the White House, ending subsidies to fossil fuel companies and, most significantly, instituting a carbon tax that would set a price on carbon for fossil fuel producers or importers starting at $15 per ton in 2017, rising to $73 per ton by 2035, and growing by 5 percent annually after that. The money would be used as a rebate for consumers and to protect frontline communities.

Sanders's carbon tax proposal became a major point of conten-
tion between him and Hillary Clinton, as he pressed her at a televised debate repeatedly, asking, "I would ask you to respond. Are
you in favor of a tax on carbon?"

She was not, part of Democrats' long-standing fear of being labeled as tax hikers.

"I want to do what we can do to actually make progress in dealing
with the crisis," she responded. "And my approach, I think, is going
to get us there faster without tying us up into political knots with a
Congress that still would not support what you are proposing."

As the Sanders forces and Clinton forces sat together at the
end of the campaign to construct the party's platform heading into
its convention in Philadelphia in July, environmental issues were
among the most vexing subjects. The Clinton camp resisted calls
for a carbon tax and declined to endorse a statement of purpose
that most fossil fuels should remain in the ground, deciding instead
to call for putting a price on emissions of carbon dioxide and other
greenhouse gases and rejecting a ban on fracking while similarly
emphasizing renewables over natural gas.

Activists were disappointed the platform stuck to vague principles rather than concrete goals but were hopeful that a President
Clinton would stick to them nonetheless.

"We assume that everyone takes it seriously because it's clearly
been the vehicle for bringing together the Sanders and Clinton
wings of the party, over very careful and detailed and elaborate
bargaining," said Bill McKibben, who was on the platform draft-
ing committee. "One assumes they mean it, but if they don't, every
demonstration that we hold for four years will have those words
written on the placards and banners."[5]

The environmental movement in the US had waxed and waned
over the years, but it hadn't been much of a potent political force,
at least not nationally. Environmental issues were just not enough
of a priority for most voters, at least compared to the economy and
public safety, and those for whom it mattered were thought to be

unpersuadable voters who were going to vote Democratic no matter what.

Climate activists were initially encouraged by the prospect of an Obama presidency, especially after eight years of a president who had been a Texas oil man. It was Obama who said in a speech on the last night of voting in the long 2008 Democratic primary, "If we are willing to work for it, and fight for it, and believe in it, then I am absolutely certain that, generations from now, we will be able to look back and tell our children that . . . this was the moment when the rise of the oceans began to slow and our planet began to heal."[6]

But as the Obama era progressed, environmentalists grew disillusioned. In 2009, the administration failed to close a deal to address climate change at a global summit in Copenhagen. Oil and gas extraction rose from the Bush years under Obama as his administration opened up more and more lands, both public and private, to drilling. Obama encouraged fracking, proposed weak rules on methane leaks, and didn't release a serious plan to combat climate change until the beginning of his second term in 2013. At the end of 2015, the Obama administration did join other nations in ratifying the Paris climate agreement, which required each of the 189 countries that signed it to address global warming by keeping the global average temperature rise in this century to well below 2 degrees Celsius above preindustrial levels.

Young activists, many of whom attended the 2015 Paris Climate Change Conference as part of a youth delegation, left disappointed even though the agreement was one of the most comprehensive environmental measures ever agreed to in an international context. The agreement, they felt, didn't move fast enough or go far enough to meet the urgency of the threat, and it left smaller and poorer island nations without enough resources or protections.

"Hurricane Sandy had already come, New York City was practically underwater, and Obama hadn't even talked about climate change," said Garrett Blad, an environmental activist who had attended the Paris talks as an organizer with SustainUS, a youth-led climate organization. Blad and others blamed this in part on the fact that Obama had received millions of dollars in donations from the oil and gas industry, something most observers just chalked up to the price of doing business in politics, but that activists saw as the reason why progress was so hard to come by.

In Paris, Blad says, "we were there, fighting on the inside, and we could see how this administration was really holding the arms of smaller, weaker countries behind their backs to make sure that the language was strong around its ambitions but weak around the actual mechanisms and financing that would allow it to be successful. They fought to make the agreement as watered down as possible. It became really clear when we were there that there was a mobilization gap, that there wasn't a movement in America to push the climate issue further."

Matthew Miles Goodrich was similarly disillusioned. He was crushed when the Copenhagen summit fell apart in 2009, when he was just a high school student in a small town in Connecticut. He went to Bowdoin College in Maine and started getting into campus activism, encouraging schools and universities to divest from fossil fuel holdings in their endowments. That effort, spearheaded by McKibben, was called 350.org, and it sprung up on several college campuses in the years after 2012. More than six hundred university and college presidents committed to reduce greenhouse gas emissions and to educate their students on the science and the importance of mitigating the effects of climate change. But only a handful of colleges and universities followed through on divestment, as schools felt obligated to maximize the return on their investments.

But winning wasn't always the point either.

"Campaigns aren't just about winning a 'yes' on divestment," the group said in a statement of purpose. "They're about telling the story of people power against the fossil fuel industry. Getting a 'yes' on divestment is a big part of that, but creating tension at a school that might be unlikely to divest tells that story, too.

"By dismantling the fossil fuel industry's social license, we can break the hold they have over our economy and governments, make way for community-led solutions to the crisis, achieve strong climate legislation, and shift the paradigm on fossil fuel dependency."

After graduation Goodrich scooted over the border to New Hampshire, getting a job with 350.org's political arm and started working on the Democratic primary between Bernie Sanders and Hillary Clinton.

Mostly that involved trying to get to talk for a few seconds with Hillary Clinton on a rope line, catching the interaction on film, and trying to get her to commit to concrete climate goals, or at least to say something mildly embarrassing. Eventually, Clinton's staff and security cottoned on to who he was, and they kept Goodrich away from the candidate as much as possible, but not before he could get one of the organizers he trained to goad Clinton into lashing out at her on camera after she asked about Sanders's allegation that she was taking money from fossil fuel interests.

"I do not have—I have money from people who work for fossil fuel companies. I am so sick—I am so sick of the Sanders campaign lying about me," Clinton said while angrily pointing her finger at the activist. "I'm sick of it."

The video went viral online, but Goodrich began to see that it wasn't quite enough. "Hillary Clinton at that time looked overwhelmingly like the next nominee," he said. "And we needed to concentrate on winning concessions from her. That was the logic. And at the time it seemed really cutting edge for the landscape that we were dealing with. We thought that if we could get Clinton on the record saying these things then we could hammer her if she then tried to reverse herself after she became the nominee."

But Goodrich and other activists also noticed something else that was afoot in that primary. Even though Sanders seemed to have galvanized progressives and young people to join his movement in droves, institutions on the left and organizations dedicated to the environment weren't set up to help him and to tap into that energy. Instead, they focused on getting Clinton to say something embarrassing on camera.

"The whole point of what we did was to push Democratic candidates in our direction, but we couldn't pivot to supporting Bernie Sanders on anything like the scale that the enthusiasm he generated warranted," Goodrich said. Part of the problem was that many in the green movement were skeptical of electoral politics and of political leaders in general. But on the other hand, Sanders showed how popular many of the ideas these activists had been promoting really were, even as they had been dismissed for years as fringe players in US politics.

"With Bernie, with Standing Rock, you saw millions of people coming out to show support," said Blad. "Talking about 'fossil fuel billionaires and how this was the issue of our time.' I think it showed the potential of a mass movement for these kinds of ideas."

The election of Trump was a devastating blow to climate activists, a repudiation in many ways of their approach to the election, and it took a hammer to their strategy of trying to push Democrats and, in particular, a Democratic administration, to the left.

There were seemingly thousands of disparate climate and environmental groups blooming at the time, but none that were directly intervening in the political process in a serious and sustained way. Sanders had nearly won, and had done so pushing their issues, but without much of a presence from environmental organizations helping him out on the ground.

And so, after the primary, a core group of a dozen or so organizers, sponsored by 350.org, started talking about how to plot a path forward. They met in various places around the country, sharing readings about social movements like the civil rights movement, the LGBT-equality movement, Occupy Wall Street, the Tea Party, and even Kony 2012, a movement to shine a spotlight on Ugandan warlord and kidnapper Joseph Kony and eventually have him arrested.

The organizers also received direction from Momentum, a group that had begun in 2013 when young activists Carlos Saavedra and

Paul Engler met at a training institute in Portland, Oregon.[7] There was, they came to realize, a missing piece in some of the activism emerging in the second Obama term. There were a lot of groups and a lot of energy, but no coordination, no sharing of best practices. They wondered, How do you get media attention? How do you organize in such a way that galvanizes people from all walks of life and lets them feel like they are a part of it? How do you tell your story? How, in other words, do you build a movement?

Momentum's trainings encouraged activists to make big, splashy protests that would attract media attention and provide arresting visuals. "Momentum teaches activists how to fuse huge, seemingly spontaneous uprisings like Occupy with traditional structures of labor unions and community organizing. That means deploying dramatic demonstrations, since a simple march or rally isn't always enough for people to pay attention, and to claim victory so the opposition can't downplay their effectiveness," wrote Tyler Kingkade in a rare profile of a group that does not try to bring attention to its work.[8] "To hear Momentum's leadership tell it, activists emerging from their training could significantly reshape politics through disruptive nonviolent protests that will chase people out of a passive middle ground, and ramp up pressure to break stalemates on issues like immigration and global warming. They disregard what is considered politically possible in favor of what would be ideal."[9]

The founders of Momentum had seen groups and even movements bubble up over the previous years, but then fade into irrelevance. They wanted their allies to build something that would last. And so they encouraged groups to create a story they wanted to tell about themselves and their cause and to think about their work as a cycle of escalation and absorption, of high-profile fights followed by organizing meetings to bring more and more people in.[10]

On election night 2016, as much of the rest of the country looked on aghast at the returns coming in, that group of a dozen or so young climate activists were gathered in a farmhouse in Lancaster, PA, trying to figure out a way to make what they saw as the existential issue of climate change relevant in American politics.

"We were watching Bernie nearly win, and Trump win, this whole debacle unfold, and no young people who were scared about the climate crisis had any role in it," said Varshini Prakash. She had been a campus divestment activist at University of Massachusetts-Amherst, but had begun to feel like her work wasn't approaching the scope of the problem. And so she and her young allies in the climate movement began to plot a way forward that would allow for a massive transformation far greater than one the election that night seemed to portend.

"As the whole rest of the country was freaking out, we were planning," she told me.[11] The group came up with what they called their DNA Guide, a plan for action, which they made public in the hopes that others would use it and join them. "Sunrise is building an army of young people to stop climate change, and create millions of good jobs in the process," they wrote on their website. "We will unite to make climate change an urgent priority across this country, end the corrupting influence of fossil fuel executives on our politics, and elect leaders who stand up for the health and wellbeing of all people."[12]

The group pegged the next election as critical to the future, both theirs and the planet's.

"It all pivots around 2018," the DNA Guide read. "Next year, politicians across the country will be running for reelection. This is our chance to make stopping climate change and creating renewable energy jobs a decisive election issue for the very first time. 2018 could be the year when it is no longer acceptable for politicians to take money from fossil fuel CEO's who are driving us to destruction. To get there, we need to build an army of thousands of young people, starting right now."

"We knew we needed to bring the climate movement into politics," said Blad. "The movement for so long had been focused on pipeline fights, or working at the UN level, or doing divestment campaigns. They were good in their own right, but they were really kind of outside of politics and not actually confronting the scale of the problem. And we kind of sat out the 2016 election that may have been the most consequential election of our lifetime."

At the dark hour of Trump's election, they picked the name "Sunrise" because it conveyed that a brighter future was in the offing, just off in the distance, and because it conveyed that the movement would be led by people not yet fully visible—that is, young people who hadn't yet engaged much in politics.

Sunrise's leaders figured that for too long the environmental movement had been focused on presenting facts on the science. These facts made them feel certain of the rightness of their position, but they didn't communicate a winning story to the public. McKibben's organization after all was named 350.org, for the parts per million of carbon dioxide in the atmosphere. His major tour of college campuses after the 2012 election was called "Do the Math." They were right on the science, but they had no story worth telling.

"The other piece of it was that the movement, and really movements on the left in general, had been too interested in a kind of purity politics," said Blad. "Organizations working on this issue insisted on being the most pure instead of creating a culture that was broadly accepted in mass culture, and that was welcoming and inviting of people who aren't 'woke Twitter,' who aren't the activists who know all the right things to say and do. And so the environmental movement and left movements in general grew smaller rather than bigger."

Sunrise tried to take a different, more welcoming approach, encouraging like-minded people to start groups of their own around the country, posting how to do so online and keeping the format simple and open. "The climate movement, and young people in particular, had no idea how to get to scale," said Prakash, who would become Sunrise's first executive director. "We needed to pass the most ambitious piece of legislation in a century, we needed a movement of millions of people but we had no idea how to do that. And we had no political power, and we knew that if we wanted to be relevant we needed to merge the strategies of protest movements and the strategies of electoral politics."

They did a study of the last five years of the environmental movement, looking over speeches and fundraising solicitations and op-eds, and realized that the environmental movement needed to be better storytellers.

"We realized we needed to talk about values," said Prakash. "We were talking about carbon and about parts-per-million, and we needed to be talking about air, water, health, the economy, things that matter to people. It's about creating a moral framework, and giving people a sense of the urgency and immediacy of this crisis but also giving them a moral framework and a sense that there can be a better future."

The experience of being in the climate movement, and seeing what other groups were doing, led the founders of Sunrise to strike out on their own, despite being in their early twenties and despite the fact that there were environmental organizations that had been doing the work for decades. It all, though, came to seem inadequate to them.

"We just had a lot of hubris, basically," said Prakash. "But the other piece of it is that when you are terrified of what the future holds, and when you have no idea whether your life will be filled with World War III or whether we will be able to avoid the worst disaster and calamity to befall humankind, you are willing to take a lot of risks. I couldn't live with myself if I had to pretend that what I was doing wasn't going to be enough to prevent the catastrophe I was so scared of. And so we set about trying to find solutions that matched the scale of the problem."

Not that there has been any good news on the climate for some time, but after the election, it got even worse. Trump promised to withdraw from the Paris Agreement that activists found to be inadequate, and to move forward on the Dakota Access Pipeline project, promises that he quickly followed through on.

In 2018, the Intergovernmental Panel on Climate Change, a group of scientists convened by the United Nations, released a report that verified what many of the critics of the Paris Agreement had said all along: unless drastic changes were made, the atmosphere would warm up by as much as 1.5 degrees Celsius, creating cascading and disastrous effects on the environment, with flooded coastlines and severe droughts that could drastically alter human life. That same year, Greta Thunberg, an unknown fifteen-year-old from Sweden, addressed a United Nations climate summit in Poland and gave a searing speech that went viral and captured the world's attention.

"You say you love your children above all else, and yet you are stealing their future in front of their very eyes," she told world leaders. "Until you start focusing on what needs to be done rather than what is politically possible, there is no hope. We cannot solve a crisis without treating it as a crisis. We need to keep fossil fuels in the ground, and we need to focus on equity. And if solutions within the system are so impossible to find, maybe we should change the system itself. We have not come here to beg world leaders to care. You have ignored us in the past, and you will ignore us again. We have run out of excuses and we are running out of time.

"We have come here to let you know that change is coming, whether you like it or not."

Sunrise decided to focus on what was right before them: the 2018 midterm elections. Although there were no age requirements, the leadership and membership of Sunrise was overwhelmingly young, and they wanted to make that a focus and a strength of the story they told. Young people at Marjory Stoneman Douglas High School in Parkland, Florida, had taken to the streets after a school shooter killed seventeen of their schoolmates. It was just the latest carnage in a nation that had grown numbly inured to such tragedies, but for once the students decided they had had enough, and they began to demand that their elected officials take measures to keep them safe.

"One thing that was becoming clear was that the people in charge have no clue what they are doing," said Goodrich. "It was time for young people to take control of the levers of power, because we had been shut out and it really seemed like we could do as good a job as anyone else."

In April 2017, tens of thousands of climate activists converged on the streets of Washington, DC, on behalf of the climate movement. It was President Trump's one hundredth day in office, and they chanted, "Resistance is here to stay, welcome to your hundredth day!" There were similar smaller marches around the country, but the newly formed Sunrise Movement did not participate. Or not in a real way, at least. Instead, they were there in their yellow T-shirts and black pants, collecting names and email addresses for use in their launch. It was a symbolic moment and showed that some of the old protest methods were ending. These kinds of pre-planned and well-publicized marches were of the past, something that captured the news cycle for a day, at most, and allowed participants to feel good about themselves. Something that impacted politics in a tangible way was more necessary.

And like any good storytellers, Sunrise made sure that the story they told had a bad guy. It wasn't Trump, necessarily, or the Republican Party, but it was fossil fuel executives who had a stranglehold on US politics. It is why the group focused first on getting candidates to pledge not to accept money from oil and gas companies. "Frankly, we needed to create an enemy," Prakash said. "And so we picked fossil fuel CEOs and the candidates they control."

"The only thing that can overcome the influence of the fossil fuel executives is a massive popular uprising to eject them and their puppets from our political system," the group wrote in its founding documents, a twelve-page memo called "The Sunrise Movement Plan: A Guide to Defeat Trump and Make Climate Change an Urgent Political Priority."

The plan read,

> Fortunately, climate action is already very popular, and people are already rising up to resist Trump's pro-billionaire, pro-pollution agenda. All we need to do as Sunrise is harness this energy and direct it towards winning real political power. It all pivots around 2018. Next year, politicians across the country will be running for reelection. This is our chance to make stopping climate change

and creating renewable energy jobs a decisive election issue for the very first time. 2018 could be the year when it is no longer acceptable for politicians to take money from fossil fuel CEO's who are driving us to destruction.

To get there, we need to build an army of thousands of young people, starting right now. Here's how we'll do it: We'll start Sunrise "hubs" in schools, houses of worship, small towns, and big cities across the country. The basic work of a Sunrise hub is simple: talk to people about climate change, and tell them about our plan to stop it. We'll go to shows, to youth groups, to high school classes, university clubs, and anywhere else where we know we'll find young people who are looking for a way to make a difference. As we talk to people, our hubs will grow, and we'll have more people to do the next round of outreach.

As we grow our hubs, we'll be collecting signatures on petitions to protect the Paris climate Accord. Trump withdrew from Paris, but state governors and legislatures can still uphold the agreement by committing to end fossil fuel pollution and create renewable energy jobs in their state. A majority of people in every single state support the Paris Accord, and we need every governor to follow our will. This popular demand gives us something tangible to talk to people about as we build towards 2018.

Facing limited resources, some of Sunrise's first actions were in New York—staging a sit-in in front of Andrew Cuomo's office and recruiting campaign fellows to work on races of the progressives who were challenging members of the moderate Independent Democratic Conference. A few of them tried to learn the tools of the trade by first working on AOC's race.

Ocasio-Cortez was still in the nascent phase of her candidacy when she tweeted, in response to a McKibben tweet about flood and mass evacuations in Florida, "Climate change is an existential threat if we ignore it, but can be an opportunity if we pursue a #GreenNewDeal. I support the latter."[13]

The Green New Deal was still a vague policy concept at the time, but a number of progressive candidates in 2018 embraced it. Many on the Left felt it was no longer a time to make small plans or for a piecemeal approach that would improve people's lives only marginally. "We wanted to do a World War II style mobilization to rebuild the economy but without the war," said Zack Exley, one of the founders of Justice Democrats and Brand New Congress and an early supporter of AOC's campaign. "Then we built new industries out of nothing, using free-market mechanisms, but with the government as a big player in the free market, and it kept going for decades around the world. It's actually a really normal thing. This is just how countries keep up. This is how countries keep from declining."

The mastermind of the Green New Deal is Rhiana Gunn-Wright, then a policy director at New Consensus, a think tank aligned with Ocasio-Cortez and founded by Exley and led by Saikat Chakrabarti, who became AOC's first chief of staff. Educated at Yale and Oxford and raised on the South Side of Chicago, Gunn-Wright knew that a twenty-first-century environmental agenda couldn't just focus on the environment; it needed to focus on jobs and infrastructure, and it needed focus on marginalized communities that were going to bear the brunt of the worst impacts of climate change. The key, she told Marie Claire magazine in a 2019 profile, is "figuring out how you create policies when you assume that no one and no place is disposable."[14]

According to Exley, the Green New Deal almost wasn't called that. The phrase had been kicking around for a while, even *New York Times* columnist Thomas Friedman used it in a piece a decade before, but it had largely been a fringe policy notion advanced mostly by Green Party candidates in the United States.[15]

Exley said that it took some selling among the activist class before they embraced the Green New Deal. For one thing, the original New Deal was a slew of government public works projects and social welfare programs, but what today's activists were calling for was something more akin to the buildup that took place during and after World War II but one that would ramp up industrialization to decarbonize the economy, not to fight the Nazis. Plus, for many young activists, the New Deal connoted discriminatory housing and employment practices, and calling it "green" suggested that it was meant strictly to improve the environment, while many saw it as a more encompassing social justice project.

"People were trying to find a different name for it, but anytime anybody said 'the Green New Deal,' journalists would write about it and say, 'Ah, I know what this is. They are talking about a sweeping economic project.' There was no other way to put it so that people would understand. Those were the three magic words that conjured something sweeping," Exley said.[16]

One of the cornerstones of the Green New Deal was a federal jobs guarantee that was bubbling up in the months and years after Clinton's defeat. A federal jobs guarantee would put all able-bodied Americans to work on critical infrastructure projects and social service needs, a proposal that would reintegrate long-term unemployed people back into the labor force and, proponents hoped, push wages higher for the already employed. Plus, it was seen as something that was more realistic than a universal basic income, an idea that had been gaining in popularity in order to combat the coming joblessness associated with increased automation.

"The key to the Green New Deal was really the federal jobs guarantee," said NoiseCat. "It was something that was starting to get talked about more and more in the 2018 primaries, and before the IPCC report of 1.5 degrees and before Greta. It was a question of, How do we piggyback climate onto more popular stuff? Could you trojan horse it through a federal jobs guarantee?"

Ocasio-Cortez's platform didn't include a tab for the "Green New Deal"—the resolution became well known after she won the primary but before she won the general election, yet her website said that Ocasio-Cortez believes we must place significant limits on carbon emissions, while investing deeply in wind, solar and other forms of renewable energy technologies. In order to address runaway global climate change, Alexandria strongly supports transitioning the United States to a carbon-free, 100% renewable energy system and a fully modernized electrical grid by 2035. She believes renewable fuels must be produced in a way that achieves our environmental and energy security goals, so we can move beyond oil responsibly in the fight against climate change. By encouraging the electrification of vehicles, sustainable home heating, distributed rooftop solar generation, and the conversion of the power grid to zero-emissions energy sources, Alexandria believes we can be 100% free of fossil fuels by 2035.

Furthermore, Alex believes in recognizing the relationship between economic stability and environmental sustainability. It's time to shift course and implement a Green New Deal—a transformation that implements structural changes to our political and financial systems in order to alter the trajectory of our environment. Right now, the economy is controlled by big corporations whose profits are dependent on the continuation of climate change. This arrangement benefits few, but comes at the detriment of our planet and all its inhabitants. Its effects are life-threatening, and are especially already felt by low-income communities, both in the U.S. and globally. Even in NY-14, areas like Throgs Neck, College Point, and City Island are being affected by erosion and rising sea levels. Rather than continue a dependency on this system that posits climate change as inherent to economic life, the Green New Deal believes that radically addressing climate change is a potential path towards a more equitable economy with increased employment and widespread financial security for all.

Interest grew in this strange new phrase after Ocasio-Cortez's remarkable victory over Joe Crowley. "Alexandria Ocasio-Cortez's climate plan is the only one that matches scientific consensus on the environment," declared *Quartz* the day after the primary. "Alexandria Ocasio-Cortez Will Be the Leading Democrat on Climate Change," added the *Huffington Post* the same day. A week later, the *New Republic* declared that Ocasio-Cortez had no less than a "Plan to Save the Planet."[17]

But after Democrats swept into power in the House of Representatives that November, enthusiasm for ambitious environmental initiatives waned. Voters in Washington State, a reliably Democratic state and one known to embrace environmental causes, decisively rejected a referendum calling for a carbon tax. A widely shared story in the Washington-insider newspaper *The Hill* in October was headlined "Dems Damp Down Hopes for Climate Change Agenda." The Democrats had succeeded by winning over moderate suburban districts that were longtime GOP strongholds, and incoming House Speaker Nancy Pelosi was urging the party to go slow.

But a week after the election, members of the Sunrise Movement arrived in Washington. They had told Ocasio-Cortez's staff that they planned to do a sit-in in Pelosi's office, and they asked if she could retweet some kind of bland statement of support for moving forward on a robust effort to combat climate change. Ocasio-Cortez responded herself, telling the group they weren't thinking big enough. She and her staff and the staff of Sunrise started working furiously over the next forty-eight hours—most of them through the night—trying to come up with something more concrete to demand from Pelosi.

They came up with calling for a House Select Committee on a Green New Deal. The night before the sit-in, hundreds of Sunrise members arrived at a DC church, dressed in identical outfits and singing. Ocasio-Cortez showed up and surprised them, alongside fellow congresswoman Rashida Tlaib, also newly elected.

Dressed immaculately in a tan suit and white blouse despite the long day of meetings she had just had, Ocasio-Cortez got up on a table and addressed the crowd. "This journey began for me at Standing Rock," she told them. "It started with us bearing witness and standing shoulder to shoulder with people willing to put their bodies and their lives on the line for our future. We are busting down the doors!"

The next morning, dozens of Sunrise members patiently lined the hallways of the Capitol, eventually, and to their surprise, getting inside Pelosi's office. TVs on the walls were turned to CNN, which was showing footage of wildfires in California, proof to them of how necessary their movement was. And then, to their surprise, Ocasio-Cortez showed up again. It was a stunning breach of protocol for a member of Congress, let alone one not yet sworn in. "This is about unity, this is about solidarity, and this is about that we have to make a better future for our kids," she told the protesters, many of them kneeling and holding signs that said "Step Up or Step Aside."

"I was terrified," Ocasio-Cortez recalled a year later in an interview.[18] "I didn't know that I was risking something huge of which I didn't quite know what it was or its contours. I learned a lot about how fear shapes the decisions of elected officials, particularly members of Congress, because it's precisely that. It's the fear of the unknown that keeps people in check because it's like, 'I know this could be bad and this could make someone mad, and I don't know exactly how they would drop the hammer on me or what hammers would be dropped. It's just too much work, and so we're just going to not rock the boat.'

"It was so stressful because it was not planned. This wasn't some big operation set up where it's like, 'Okay, we're going to come down to DC at this time. On day two, we're going to do this.' I showed up and these activists asked me to visit them at this church that they were sleeping at the night before the protest. I went and they asked me to join them at the sit-in. The idea of that was terrifying, but at the same time I'm looking at fourteen- and fifteen-year-olds in the face that are willing to get arrested and not go to college or risk their college admissions for climate action and no one was paying attention to this issue. Even for those that were, the scale that they're paying attention to this issue was basically a form of denialism. We had to really do something huge to shift the frame and center this conversation, particularly on an issue that is notoriously ignored. It just felt like the right thing to do."

Protests in Washington are an everyday occurrence, but this one, in the next Speaker's office after a huge victory, will forever be remembered as one of the most meaningful in history. Sunrise had figured out that there was an ongoing media narrative about the old guard Democratic establishment and the impatient newcomers, and they harnessed the one figure who had come to embody that fight for their purpose.

After the protest, the group continued to make a name for itself by most notably sitting in California senator Dianne Feinstein's office, a sit-in that allowed them to capture Feinstein lecturing the young protesters about how they didn't understand how the Senate worked. The footage was so powerful that nearly every Democrat running for president in 2020 endorsed the Green New Deal, something that would have been unthinkable even two years before. Ocasio-Cortez, working alongside Senator Edward Markey of Massachusetts, made a Green New Deal her first major legislative push. An early draft of the legislation was mistakenly put online, and so the Green New Deal became an object of mockery on the right, as Fox News and others accused the new Democratic star of wanting to ban cows and airplane travel, but a majority of the Democratic conference supported it, and it shifted the paradigm of the environmental debate from being about scarcity and sacrifice to being about a brighter, wealthier, and cleaner future.

"Until then the most ambitious climate plans were a carbon tax here or a biodiesel thing there," Ocasio-Cortez said. "But the most ambitious plans were in the billions, and this is a one-trillion-dollar scale, massive infrastructure issue. It was the space where we, as an office, could shift public policy the most."

But it wasn't just about policy for her. A group of earnest and ambitious young people had come to Washington asking for change. And for once, they had someone willing to listen. "It's how I try to approach legislating and approach my job, which is in response to movements," Ocasio-Cortez said. "That movement pressed and called to action. And it was my responsibility to respond."

EPILOGUE
November 2020

I sit here at the end of an unsettled political season. The election is over, Joe Biden has won, Donald Trump has refused to concede, and Democrats sustained surprising losses in the House and Senate and in the states. In big metropolitan areas, meanwhile, the party's left flank continued to exert their influence, knocking off longtime Democratic incumbents down-ballot.

The party is engaged in one of its time-honored post-election practices, blaming the other faction for the losses incurred and crediting its own for the victories, and it is, truly, uncertain how all of this will be resolved.

But throughout this long election cycle, Alexandria Ocasio-Cortez has been inescapable. She boosted Bernie Sanders at the critical moments of his campaign, endorsing him before 25,000 people at a park in Queens and campaigning for him in front of similarly sized crowds across the country. After he bowed out, Ocasio-Cortez was the only political figure in America besides the two running for president who consistently commanded the public's attention. For Donald Trump, she was the leader of "AOC plus three," a public menace who, merely by the invocation of her name, would become a stand-in for a rising generation that was more diverse than the one before it, more liberal, and, more to the point, coming after the privilege of middle-class communities.

Democrats didn't embrace her much either. Joe Biden mostly tried to keep Ocasio-Cortez at bay, declining to campaign alongside her out of fear that she would spook those very same voters. Her most prominent campaign appearance came when she put forward Sanders's name for the nomination at the Democratic National Convention. It was a ninety-second speech, one in which she discussed many of the themes of this book, paying tribute to the people and movements who helped make her possible:

> a mass people's movement working to establish 21st century social, economic, and human rights . . . a movement striving to recognize and repair the wounds of racial injustice, colonization, misogyny, and homophobia, and to propose and build reimagined systems of immigration and foreign policy that turn away from the violence and xenophobia of our past; a movement that realizes the unsustainable brutality of an economy that rewards explosive inequalities of wealth for the few at the expense of long-term stability for the many, and who organized an historic, grassroots campaign to reclaim our democracy.[1]

As with all things AOC-related, a run-of-the-mill appearance became spun into a days-long controversy: Why was she only given ninety seconds? Why didn't she mention Biden? Is the party turning its back on the young?—never mind that her speech was standard fare for someone placing the party's runner-up into nomination.

But then again, in the last three years, it has always been thus for Alexandria Ocasio-Cortez. For two years, she has served in Washington with a spotlight on her unlike any seen before for a rookie lawmaker. Her Washington, DC, office has become a place of pilgrimage, as thousands of visitors from around the country leave supportive Post-it notes on the wall outside her door. Tourists come and pay respect to her old bar off Manhattan's Union Square. Normal political practices, like giving speeches or questioning witnesses at hearings or giving cable TV interviews are, when performed by

AOC, blown up into massive news events. When a politician can command a news cycle like this, we say that they make their own weather; Ocasio-Cortez is an atmosphere all to herself, and it has become impossible to look away.

This book ended at the beginning. It tells the story of the forces that powered the rise of Alexandria Ocasio-Cortez but leaves off just at the point when she had arrived. In the months after Ocasio-Cortez was sworn into Congress, she busted out of the bounds of being merely a political figure to being a cultural one. She sat for glossy magazine spreads, was interviewed by the actress Kerry Washington. She appeared on *Desus & Mero*, the hit Showtime show, taking the two comedians around her Bronx neighborhood, including a stop at her favorite bodega for a bacon, egg, and cheese sandwich and mixing up drinks for them as a throwback to her bartender days. She became a judge on *RuPaul's Drag Race*. There are action figures in her likeness and comic books that tell her story. When she name-checked her favorite lipstick brand on Twitter, it sold out immediately. In July of 2020, after a right-wing congressman, Ted Yoho of Florida, called her "a fucking bitch" on the Capitol steps,[2] then issued a non-apology in which he mentioned that he was the father of daughters, Ocasio-Cortez took to the floor of the House to excoriate him: "And so what I believe is that having a daughter does not make a man decent. Having a wife does not make a decent man. Treating people with dignity and respect makes a decent man."[3] Months later, on Ocasio-Cortez's thirty-first birthday, Gen Z women took to TikTok, putting on makeup—including her signature red lipstick—while lip-synching her floor rebuttal, stopping at the line "I am here because I have to show my parents that I am their daughter and that they did not raise me to accept abuse from men." In the weeks before the election, she played *Among Us*, an online multiplayer game, on Twitch, a streaming platform. More than 430,000 viewers tuned in, the largest audience ever on the platform, and she sent more voters to IWillVote.com, the Democratic National Committee's voter registration and information site, than had ever gone there previously.[4]

On the right, it was the same, but through the looking glass. One 2019 study, by the liberal watchdog group Media Matters for America, found that Ocasio-Cortez was mentioned *seventy-six times a day* on Fox News and Fox Business, or nearly three times per hour, and that not a day went by when she wasn't mentioned.[5] It wasn't just Trump who tried to tag his opponent with AOC's policies but also Republicans in races around the country and up and down the ballot who warned that their Democratic opponent would be in thrall to the first-term lawmaker from the Bronx and Queens. When, a week after the 2020 election, John Thune, the number-two Republican in the Senate, told reporters that the results were "a rejection of the far-left, Schumer, Pelosi, AOC agenda,"[6] Ocasio-Cortez responded, "If I were actually as all-commandingly powerful as Republicans say I am, everybody in this country would have guaranteed healthcare by now," in a tweet that (as usual) garnered hundreds of thousands of retweets and likes.[7] "Alas, I'm just a first term Congresswoman, standing in front of a government, asking it to love working people."

The exchange crystallized how Ocasio-Cortez came to dominate this moment. It is not just that her haters use her as a stand-in for the rising progressive generation, or that her supporters flocked to her charisma and cool. Ocasio-Cortez cultivated this space, clapping back at her critics and meeting her fans where they were, whether it was on a video-game platform or in the pages of *Vogue*. She is the first member of Congress truly fluent in social media, and one of the first to recognize that politics has become another pop cultural pursuit, and that for her message to succeed it has to first reach people. She has become the most prominent spokesperson for left politics in at least a quarter century, and in doing so, she has become surely the most significant political figure of her age besides Donald Trump, despite sitting at the furthest back of the back benches of the House of Representatives.

In her first term in office, Ocasio-Cortez openly feuded with House Speaker Nancy Pelosi, nearly single-handedly kept Amazon from building a new campus in New York by coming out against it (even though, as a federal lawmaker, she had no say over the matter, and HQ2 was not even in her district), and was the lone Democrat to vote against funding the government because it meant funding Immigrations and Customs Enforcement. She had promised to carry to Washington the voices of the activists who got her there, and it is hard to argue that she failed to do so.

Still, over the summer of 2020, on a phone call with activists and organizers from Democratic Socialists of America, Ocasio-Cortez pushed for her fellow travelers on the left to work to increase their coalition. "I think it's incredibly important that we do all of this with an open posture," Ocasio-Cortez said in the call, a recording of which I obtained. "This is not a contest about who knows more. This is about making sure that we are really reaching out and making this the most inviting, exciting, and, frankly, promising way of politics that is most inspiring to the most people in this country. And that is really the posture that we need to have or else we will not win. So it's possible to be both be revolutionary and also create an open enough posture where people all across the country are willing to buy in.

"We should not replicate the capitalist politics of domination and ownership upon others," she added. "We are part of a larger community, and we have to build that coalition in order to win."

She told the group that fighting against the powers that be was difficult: "The emotional component is a huge part of the political component. We have these votes where 99 percent of the party is voting one way and 1 percent or less are voting the other way," but she added that true change would come from them. "The critique that folks on the left have of folks in elected office, and particularly of democratic socialists in elected office, is that we are not doing every single possible thing in the universe, and that is because electoral politics simply cannot do what mass movements can. We have to be very aware of what zone we're in and make sure that we are operating on all cylinders, on an electoral cylinder, on a mass movement cylinder and revolutionary cylinders as we restructure power," she said, adding that being a member of Congress "is not the only way to make change. It's difficult. It's frustrating. You have to deal with a lot of neoliberal trash, and it wears on your soul. And if there's anything that's convinced me that electoral politics is not enough, that it is necessary but not sufficient for wholesale change, it has been being an elected official. This is not the only way to make change, and we need to do so much more than just electoral politics."

It is hard to know where Ocasio-Cortez, or where the movement that propelled her rise, will go from here. Activism tends to increase, on either side of the political aisle, when your party is out of power. It very much remains to be seen if Justice Democrats, Democratic Socialists of America, Indivisible, or some of the other groups and outlets featured in these pages are able to keep up their energy and enrollment in the years to come. After the 2020 election, when Democrats lost seats in the House of Representatives and failed to deliver the electoral repudiation of Trump many hoped for, many in the party blamed AOC. With the white-hot light of the public's attention on her, she pushed for policies that, in this telling, turned off the vast middle. She continued to embrace the democratic socialist label. After a series of summer protests about police brutality, she joined activists in calling for defunding the police. As conservatives warned against socialized medicine, she called for Medicare for All. As the Republicans said Ocasio-Cortez wanted to ban cows and air travel, she continued to push for a Green New Deal.

A number of candidates endorsed by Ocasio-Cortez won election this fall, giving her a kind of clout on contested floor votes that she lacked before, but it certainly looks from this vantage point that Ocasio-Cortez, and the movement she leads, are at a low ebb. Democrats are trying to cling to slender majorities, and the dysfunctional nature of our political geography limits the power of young people clustered together on the coasts and in dense urban areas. Establishment Democrats are blaming her and her allies in the so-called Squad specifically for pushing the party past its ideological moorings.

There is some truth to this. The nation is far to the right of Ocasio-Cortez and of the many organizers who make up this book. And while there have always been left-wing members of Congress, none have been able to command the public's attention like she has before or have cultivated an audience in quite the same way. And so Ocasio-Cortez complicates the Democratic coalition in a way that may be hard to reconcile in the future, pushing it ideologically beyond a realm in which it can continue to cohere.

It doesn't necessarily have to be this way, but first Ocasio-Cortez and her allies have to decide what they want. As many were quoted saying in the pages of this book, for years the Left has been afraid of seizing power. They have preferred marches and talks and tweets, and have avoided the hard and necessary work of politics. The presidency of Donald Trump changed this, got the American Left engaged, and they gained a major foothold with Ocasio-Cortez, someone who carried their message into the mainstream of American politics. Whether they are satisfied with a mere foothold or want something more, the coming years will show.

ACKNOWLEDGMENTS

This book began, as so many good ideas do, on the blacktop playground of a New York City public school. It was the International Dinner for my kids' school, an event where the parents, who come from dozens of countries around the world, cook for the community and raise money for the PTA, and where Will Sweeney, a political activist and, like me, a neighborhood dad, first suggested I do a book on Alexandria Ocasio-Cortez and then, like good political actors everywhere, wouldn't stop talking to me about it until I actually sat down and did it.

Jane Dystel, my agent, was a coconspirator in this endeavor from the start and an incredibly patient teacher to this bewildered student of how the book publishing world really works. I am grateful to Michael Wolraich, a terrific writer in his own right, for introducing me to her and for Michael's semi-regular "Writers and Beers" meet-ups, which for years have been a great place to talk about ideas and the work with like-minded scribes. Gayatri Patnaik, my editor at Beacon, was a constant source of encouragement and advice, a joy to work with, and I couldn't have asked for a better partner on this project.

Suffice to say, this book would not have happened were it not for the participation of dozens and dozens of young activists who sat with me in coffee shops or spoke with me over the phone to tell me about their work. There are too many to list here, and their names, except when they asked them not to be, are in the book itself. In a world that is full of distractions and where it can seem like there's a conspiracy to keep people from getting engaged, they knock on doors, organize their neighborhoods, and fight like hell to make the world they want come into being. They do so often with little recognition and less pay, and, although I don't always agree with their ideas or their strategy, I admire them immensely. They are the building blocks of our democracy.

This book is in part the story of a place. Seven years ago, I moved with my family to Jackson Heights, New York, a community that is the heart of Ocasio-Cortez country and one of the most diverse neighborhoods on the planet. It is also home to a remarkable collection of writers and journalists, many of whom provided inspiration and commiseration during this project when I would venture out bleary-eyed from my study yearning for human contact and a dose of media gossip. I am grateful to have in my life David Goodman of the *New York Times*, Mitra Kalita of CNN, and Jessica Pressler, lately of *Vanity Fair*, to talk shop with.

When I showed up at the steps of the Columbia University Graduate School of Journalism fifteen years ago, I arrived with a surfeit of confidence and a deficit of knowledge and ability. There, Dale Maharidge taught me how to report and write, and Dan Janison of *Newsday* and the late, great Wayne Barrett of the *Village Voice* showed me the ins and outs of the local political scene, one I have never really left. Alisa Solomon, a theater critic and the director of the Arts and Culture journalism concentration there, is one of my journalistic heroes, someone who brings a keen eye and a fierce sense of justice to everything she does, and someone whom I am lucky to consider a friend. I returned to Columbia years later to co-teach a course in political theory and journalism with Alexander Stille and Nicholas Lemann, and I surely learned more than I taught there. This book, in part, comes out of many of the classroom discussions we were engaged in there.

Doing this work has been the thrill of a lifetime, and I am grateful to everyone who has allowed me to do it, including Tim Teeman of the *Daily Beast*, the late John Homans and Michael Calderone of *Vanity Fair*, Aaron Gell of *Medium*, Paula Szuchman, now of the *New York Times*, and Kyle Pope and Elizabeth Spiers, both formerly of the much missed *New York Observer*. Marisa Carroll and Jebediah Reed of *New York Magazine* and Steve Heuser of *Politico Magazine* are some of the finest editors I have ever had the pleasure of working with, and in this business of word production, I actually don't have any to express my gratitude to them. I am living a dream.

My parents, Barrett and Laura Freedlander, were, I am sure, the first people to buy this book and the people who instilled in me a love of reading and writing and talking politics. I am very lucky to have siblings like Jed Freedlander and La Scheu (and their spouses, Bea de la Torre and Justin Scheu), whom I can consider friends, and luckier still to consider my dear friends as family, among them Irene Balakrishnan, Cynthia Nagendra, Adam Machado, Ben Cooper, Bruce Wallace, and Marc Gilman. All of them knew me well enough to know not to ask too often about the progress of my book, which is all I can really ask of them, and to provide laughs and distraction whenever both were needed. David Reid, the author of *The Brazen Age*, was one of the first people I knew to show me what the writer's life was like and has been an unending and enthusiastic champion of my work.

This book was written under difficult circumstances, including an apartment move in the middle of it and, later, a global pandemic that closed schools and sent my daughters, Claribel and Rosa, home for the duration of one school year and the beginning of the next. I missed them immensely during the long months of writing this book, and my only hope is that it one day makes them proud of a father who loves them with his entire heart.

They are lucky, though, to have had with them for this time and for all time a mother like my wife, Lily Saint, who bore the brunt of these cataclysmic disruptions with a grace and wit that she brings to everything she does. She is a brilliant scholar and a loving partner, and this book would not have been close to possible without her.

NOTES

INTRODUCTION

1. Matthew Miles Goodrich, author interview, April 2020.

2. Holmes Lybrand, "Fact Check: Did Sanders Win More Young Voters in 2016 Than Clinton and Trump Combined?," CNN.com, February 27, 2019, https://www.cnn.com/2019/02/26/politics/fact-check-bernie-sanders-town-hall-youth-vote/index.html.

3. "Iowa Entrance Polls," *New York Times*, February 1, 2016, https://www.nytimes.com/interactive/2016/02/01/us/elections/iowa-democrat-poll.html.

4. Susan Page and Paul Singer, "USA TODAY/Rock the Vote Poll: Millennials' Agenda for the Next President," *USA Today*, updated January 11, 2016, https://www.usatoday.com/story/news/politics/elections/2016/01/11/poll-millennials-agenda-president-rock-the-vote-republican-trump-sanders-democrat/78556154.

5. "Daily Survey: Socialism," YouGov, August 1–2, 2018, https://d25d2506sfb94s.cloudfront.net/cumulus_uploads/document/oltegcolu7/tabs_YG_Socialism_20180801.pdf.

6. "US Attitudes toward Socialism, Communism, and Collectivism," Victims of Communism Memorial Foundation, October 2019, annual poll, https://www.victimsofcommunism.org/2019-annual-poll.

7. David Tigabu, "Socialism No Longer a Dirty Word in American Political Discourse," Public Religion Research Institute, January 3, 2019, 2018 American Value Survey, https://www.prri.org/spotlight/socialism-no-longer-a-dirty-word-in-american-political-discourse.

8. Tigabu, "Socialism No Longer a Dirty Word."

9. Sean McElwee and Colin McAuliffe, *Progressives Control the Future* (Data for Progress, June 14, 2020), https://www.dataforprogress.org/blog/6/14/progressives-control-the-future.

10. McElwee and McAuliffe, *Progressives Control the Future.*

11. McElwee and McAuliffe, *Progressives Control the Future.*

CHAPTER 1: SANDY

1. "Alexandria Ocasio-Cortez Remarks at 2011 Boston University Martin Luther King Jr., Celebration," posted October 3, 2018, YouTube, https://www.youtube.com/watch?v=OEKPoAml8Hk.

2. Boston University, "BU Alumna Wins Upset Congressional Primary in New York City," Boston University Federal Relations, June 27, 2018, https://www.bu.edu/federal/2018/06/27/bu-alumna-wins-upset-congressional-primary-in-new-york-city.

3. Boston University, "BU Alumna Wins Upset."

4. Alexandria Ocasio-Cortez, "Healthcare in the Bush," *Culture Shock*, October 29, 2009 http://blogs.bu.edu/aocasio/2009/10/29/healthcare-in-the-bush.

5. Hilary Cadigan, "Alexandria Ocasio-Cortez Learned Her Most Important Lessons from Restaurants," *Bon Appétit*, November 7, 2018, https://www.bonappetit.com/story/alexandria-ocasio-cortez-lessons-from-restaurants.

6. "Niger Program to Resume in Fall," *Daily Free Press*, March 18, 2010, https://dailyfreepress.com/2010/03/18/niger-program-to-resume-in-fall.

7. *Culture Shock*, Boston University blog, https://web.archive.org/web/20100224085549, http://bucultureshock.com, accessed June 2020, site now discontinued.

8. *Culture Shock*, Boston University.

9. *ICE Workplace Raids: Their Impact on U.S. Children, Families and Communities, Hearing Before the Subcommittee on Workforce Protections, Committee on Education and Labor*, 110th Cong. (May 20, 2008), https://www.govinfo.gov/content/pkg/CHRG-110hhrg42334/html/CHRG-110hhrg42334.htm.

10. Jenna Johnson, "College Roadtrip: Boston," Campus Overload Blog, *Washington Post*, March 1, 2010, https://web.archive.org/web/20170915034822/http://voices.washingtonpost.com/campus-overload/2010/03/college_roadtrip_boston.html, accessed June 2020, site now discontinued.

11. Tovia Smith, "College Students React to Bin Laden's Death," WBUR News, May 3, 2011, https://www.wbur.org/npr/135963042/college-students-react-to-bin-ladens-death

12. Dave Mosher, "Alexandria Ocasio-Cortez, the 28-Year-Old Who Defeated a Powerful House Democrat, Has an Asteroid Named After Her—Here's Why," *Business Insider*, June 28, 2018, https://www.businessinsider.com/alexandria-ocasio-cortez-asteroid-2018-6.

13. NHI Podcast, Episode 7, https://anchor.fm/nhi-podcasts/episodes/NHI-Notables-Ep-7---Alexandria-Ocasio-Cortez--NATLDZ-05--Candidate-for-the-U-S--Congress-ehp7i1.

14. Patrick Wall, "New Bill Would Double Tax Breaks for Startups," DNAinfo, August 21, 2012, https://www.dnainfo.com/new-york/20120821 /hunts-point/new-bill-would-double-tax-breaks-for-start-ups/slideshow /233645/#slide-1.

15. Megan O'Neill Melle, "Want to Get Paid What You're Worth? Claire Wasserman and the Ladies Get Paid Network Are Here to Help," *Parade*, January 29, 2020, https://parade.com/987623/meganoneill/ladies -get-paid.

CHAPTER 2: THE DISTRICT

1. Josh Barbanel, "NYC Housing Prices Have Surpassed Pre-Crisis Peak in 2006," *Wall Street Journal*, September 18, 2018, https://www.wsj.com/articles /nyc-housing-prices-have-surpassed-pre-crisis-peak-in-2006-1537261200.

2. Alexandria Ocasio-Cortez, "Today I wore my father's favorite watch to the Women's March on Washington," Facebook, January 21, 2017.

3. Women's March Statement of Purpose, https://actionnetwork.org /events/womens-march-washington-dc-httpbitly2hkji4l?source=widget.

4. Leah Greenberg, interview by Matthew Yglesias, "Movement Build- ing in the Trump Era," *Weeds*, December 6, 2019, https://www.stitcher.com /podcast/voxs-the-weeds/e/65826586.

5. Ezra Levin, Twitter, @ezralevin, December 14, 2016.

6. David Freedlander, "The Democrats' Culture Divide," *Politico*, No- vember/December 2018, https://www.politico.com/magazine/story/2018 /10/30/democratic-party-culture-divide-wars-working-class-blue-collar -221913.

7. Jelani Cobb, "The Matter of Black Lives," *New Yorker*, March 7, 2016, https://www.newyorker.com/magazine/2016/03/14/where-is-black -lives-matter-headed.

8. Aislinn Pulley, "Black Struggle Is Not a Sound Bite: Why I Refused to Meet with President Obama," *Truthout*, February 28, 2016, https:// truthout.org/articles/black-struggle-is-not-a-sound-bite-why-i-refused-to -meet-with-president-obama.

9. Violet Ikonomova, "Meet the Detroit Filmmakers Helping Promote Progressive Candidates Around the Country," *Detroit Metro Times*, June 12, 2018, https://www.metrotimes.com/news-hits/archives/2018/06/12 /these-detroit-filmmakers-are-helping-promote-progressive-candidates -around-the-country.

10. Diana Budds, "The Brilliance of Alexandria Ocasio-Cortez's Bold Campaign Design," *Vox*, July 2, 2018, https://www.vox.com/policy-and -politics/2018/7/2/17519414/ocasio-cortez-campaign-design-campaign -posters-tandem-branding.

11. Reddit AMA, archived here: https://www.reddit.com/r/SandersFor President/comments/6ftvhu/hey_reddit_i_am_alexandria_ocasiocortez_us/

CHAPTER 3: HER REVOLUTION

1. David Weigel, "Bernie Sanders Says More Than 200,000 People Have Signed Up to Help His White House Bid," *Bloomberg*, May 6, 2015, https://www.bloomberg.com/news/articles/2015-05-06/bernie-sanders-says -more-than-200-000-people-have-signed-up-to-help-his-white-house-bid.

2. Darren Samuelsohn, "Bernie's Army of Coders," *Politico*, February 18, 2016, https://www.politico.com/magazine/story/2016/02/bernie-sanders -army-of-coders-2016-213647.

3. Danny Freeman, "Sanders Brings His Political Revolution Pitch to the Bronx," NBC News, March 31, 2016, https://www.nbcnews.com/politics /2016-election/sanders-brings-his-political-revolution-pitch-bronx-n548891.

4. Sanders for President subreddit, https://www.i.reddit.com/r/Sanders ForPresident/comments/4bq3no/urgent_people_in_ny_pa_and_md_are _reporting_that.

5. Emily Atkin and Kira Lerner, "New Yorkers File Emergency Lawsuit to Give Voting Rights Back to 3.2 Million People," *ThinkProgress*, April 18, 2016, https://archive.thinkprogress.org/new-yorkers-file-emergency -lawsuit-to-give-voting-rights-back-to-3-2-million-people-3335da1dc56b.

6. "8th Anniversary of #OccupyWallStreet," Adbusters, https://www .adbusters.org/campaigns/8th-anniversary-of-occupywallstreet, accessed September 14, 2020.

7. "The Situation Room," CNN.com, October 6, 2011, http://www .cnn.com/TRANSCRIPTS/1110/06/sitroom.02.html.

8. Gregory Krieg, "Occupy Wall Street Rises Up for Sanders," CNN .com, April 13, 2016, https://www.cnn.com/2016/04/13/politics/occupy -wall-street-bernie-sanders-new-york-primary.

9. Suzy Khimm, "Bernie Sanders's Grassroots Army Is Passionate. But Can They Get Organized?," July 14, 2015, https://newrepublic.com /article/122284/bernie-sanderss-grassroots-army-passionate-disorganized.

10. The People for Bernie, https://peopleforbernie.com, accessed September 14, 2020.

11. Kate Aronoff and Ethan Corey, "Welcome to the Next Incarnation of the Bernie Sanders Campaign," *In These Times*, September 12, 2016, https://inthesetimes.com/article/19438/whose-revolution-the-next -incarnation-of-the-bernie-sanders-campaign-faces.

CHAPTER 4: THE LEFT OF THE POSSIBLE

1. Ryan Smith, "As Many as Five Socialists Could Join the City Council after Election Successes Tuesday," *Chicago Sun-Times*, February 27, 2019, https://chicago.suntimes.com/2019/2/27/18348086/as-many-as -5-socialists-could-join-city-council-after-election-successes-tuesday; James O'Toole, "Meet the Marxist Behind Seattle's Wage Hike," CNN, June 24, 2014, https://money.cnn.com/2014/06/24/news/economy/seattle -marxist-minimum-wage/index.html.

2. Michael Lerner, "Reflections on NAM," *Works and Days 55/56,* vol. 28 (Spring/Fall 2010), http://www.worksanddays.net/2010/File04 .Lerner.pdf.

3. Lerner, "Reflections on NAM."

4. Lerner, "Reflections on NAM."

5. Lerner, "Reflections on NAM."

6. "Socialist Party Now the Social Democrats, U.S.A.," *New York Times,* December 31, 1972.

7. Laurie Johnston, "Young Socialists Support Meany," *New York Times,* December 31, 1972.

8. Joseph M. Schwartz, "A History of Democratic Socialists of America 1971–2017," Democratic Socialists of America website, July 2017, https://www.dsausa.org/about-us/history.

CHAPTER 5: THE CIVIL WAR TO COME

1. Open Secrets, "Reelection Rates Over the Years," OpenSecrets.org, https://www.opensecrets.org/overview/reelect.php, accessed July 31, 2020.

2. David Ramsey, "Mahony Slams Womack for Calling Haiti and African Nations 'Depraved': 'Steve Womack Is Trafficking in Racist Comments,'" *Arkansas Blog, Arkansas Times,* January 13, 2018, https://arktimes .com/arkansas-blog/2018/01/13/mahony-slams-womack-for-calling-haiti -and-african-nations-depraved-steve-womack-is-trafficking-in-racist -comments.

3. Ellen Cranley, "These Are the 130 Current Members of Congress Who Have Doubted or Denied Climate Change," *Business Insider,* August 29, 2019, https://www.businessinsider.com/climate-change-and-republicans -congress-global-warming-2019-2#california-5.

4. Abby Zimmardi, "Steve Womack Faces Criticism at Town Hall Meeting," *Arkansas Traveler,* September 1, 2019, http://www.uatrav.com /news/article_96e14d3a-cd1a-11e9-88e5-fb2bde17b960.html.

5. Erin Duffin, "Household Income Distribution in the United States in 2018," Statista, September 24, 2019, https://www.statista.com/statistics /203183/percentage-distribution-of-household-income-in-the-us.

6. Seung Min Kim, "Cantor Loss Kills Immigration Reform," *Politico,* June 10, 2014, https://www.politico.com/story/2014/06/2014-virginia -primary-eric-cantor-loss-immigration-reform-107697.

7. David Freedlander, "There Is Going to Be a War Within the Party. We Are Going to Lean Into It," *Politico Magazine,* February 4, 2019.

CHAPTER 6: THE STORYTELLERS

1. Robert P. Baird, "The ABCs of *Jacobin*," *Columbia Journalism Review,* January 2, 2019, https://www.cjr.org/special_report/the-abcs-of -jacobin-socialist-magazine.php.

2. Bhaskar Sunkara, "Introducing Jacobin," *Jacobin*, January 1, 2011, https://jacobinmag.com/2011/01/introducing-jacobin.

3. Sunkara, "Introducing Jacobin."

4. Aida Chávez and Ryan Grim, "A Primary Against the Machine: A Bronx Activist Looks to Dethrone Joseph Crowley, the King of Queens," *Intercept*, May 22, 2018, https://theintercept.com/2018/05/22/joseph -crowley-alexandria-ocasio-cortez-new-york-primary/.

5. Chávez and Grim, "A Primary Against the Machine."

6. Chávez and Grim, "A Primary Against the Machine."

7. Ryan Grim, "Joe Crowley Complains His Primary Opponent, Alexandria Ocasio-Cortez, Is Making This Race 'About Race,'" *Intercept*, June 9, 2018, https://theintercept.com/2018/06/09/joe-crowley-alexandria -ocasio-cortez.

8. Grim, "Joe Crowley Complains."

9. Ryan Grim, author interview, November 2019.

10. "Alexandria Ocasio-Cortez Talks to Glenn Greenwald About the Democratic Party and the 2018 Midterms," *Intercept*, June 12, 2018, YouTube, https://www.youtube.com/watch?v=zuoKLLLpiuE.

11. Lee Fang, "How People Close to Joe Crowley Have Gotten Rich While the Queens Boss Has Risen in Congress," *Intercept*, June 14, 2018, https://theintercept.com/2018/06/14/joe-crowley-congress-new-york.

12. Ryan Grim, "MoveOn Endorses Democratic Primary Challenger to the Potential Next Speaker of the House," *Intercept*, June 18, 2018, https://theintercept.com/2018/06/18/joe-crowley-moveon-endorses -primary-challenger-to-the-potential-next-speaker-of-the-house.

13. Zaid Jilani, "How a Ragtag Group of Socialist Filmmakers Produced One of the Most Viral Campaign Ads of 2018," *Intercept*, June 5, 2018, https://theintercept.com/2018/06/05/ocasio-cortez-new-york-14th -district-democratic-primary-campaign-video.

14. Briahna Gray, "Two Very Different Democrats, Joe Crowley and Alexandria Ocasio-Cortez, Squared Off in Debate Friday Night," *Intercept*, June 16, 2018, https://theintercept.com/2018/06/16/two-very-different -democrats-joe-crowley-and-alexandria-ocasio-cortez-squared-off-in -debate-friday-night.

15. Glenn Greenwald, "The Democratic Party's 2018 View of Identity Politics Is Confusing, and Thus Appears Cynical and Opportunistic," *Intercept*, June 12, 2018, https://theintercept.com/2018/06/12/the-democratic -partys-2018-view-of-identity-politics-is-confusing-and-thus-appears -cynical-and-opportunistic.

16. Glenn Greenwald, Laura Poitras, and Jeremy Scahill, "Welcome to the Intercept," *Intercept*, February 10, 2014, https://theintercept.com /2014/02/10/welcome-intercept.

17. Ryan Grim, author interview, November 2019.

18. Amanda Whiting, "Cenk Uygur Just Might Be the Future of Liberal Media," *Washingtonian*, September 12, 2019, https://www.washingtonian .com/2018/09/12/cenk-uygur-future-liberal-media.

19. Jon Levine, "'Young Turks' Founder Cenk Uygur Apologizes for 'Ugly,' 'Insensitive' Old Blog Posts (Exclusive)," *Wrap*, December 21, 2017, https://www.thewrap.com/young-turks-cenk-uygur-blog-breasts -women-flawed.

20. Michael Finnegan, "Bernie Sanders Retracts Endorsement of Californian Who Defends Crude Sex Ratings of Women" *Los Angeles Times* December 13, 2019.

CHAPTER 7: THE GREEN NEW WORLD

1. Nicky Woolf, "North Dakota Oil Pipeline Protesters Stand Their Ground: 'This Is Sacred Land,'" *Guardian*, August 29, 2016, https://www .theguardian.com/us-news/2016/aug/29/north-dakota-oil-pipeline-protest -standing-rock-sioux.

2. Alexandria Ocasio-Cortez, "Social instability is a direct result of wealth inequality," Facebook, November 9, 2016.

3. Alexandria Ocasio-Cortez, "Road to Standing Rock Day 2," Facebook Live, December 20, 2016, https://www.facebook.com/alexandria .ocasiocortez/videos/10207606571147247.

4. Eric Holthaus, "Meet Julian Brave NoiseCat—the 26-Year-Old Shaping US Climate Policy," *Correspondent*, December 3, 2019, https:// thecorrespondent.com/152/meet-julian-brave-noisecat-the-26-year-old -shaping-us-climate-policy/20122769128-6ac4dd6a.

5. Phil McKenna, "Democrats Embrace Price on Carbon While Clinton Steers Clear of Carbon Tax," *InsideClimate News*, July 15, 2016, https://insideclimatenews.org/news/14072016/democratic-party-embrace -carbon-price-tax-hillary-clinton-bernie-sanders.

6. "Barack Obama's Remarks in St. Paul," transcript, *New York Times*, June 3, 2008, https://www.nytimes.com/2008/06/03/us/politics/03text -obama.html.

7. Tyler Kingkade, "These Activists Are Training Every Movement That Matters," *Vice*, November 18, 2019, https://www.vice.com/en_us /article/8xw3ba/these-activists-are-training-every-movement-that-matters -v26n4.

8. Kingkade, "These Activists Are Training."

9. Kingkade, "These Activists Are Training."

10. Rebecca Leber, "Climate Change Is Finally Having a Political Moment," *Mother Jones*, December 2, 2019, https://www.motherjones.com /politics/2019/12/climate-change-is-finally-having-a-political-moment -thats-no-accident.

11. Varshini Prakash, author interview, September 2020.

12. Sunrise Movement, https://www.sunrisemovement.org/about, accessed September 14, 2020.

13. Alexandria Ocasio-Cortez, Twitter, September 9, 2017, https://twitter.com/aoc/status/906627774168924161?lang=en.

14. Karen L. Smith-Janssen, "The Architect Behind Alexandria Ocasio-Cortez's Green New Deal Has a Plan to Save the Planet—and All of Us," *Marie Claire*, October 4, 2019, https://www.marieclaire.com/politics/a29326190/green-new-deal-architect-rhiana-gunn-wright.

15. Thomas Friedman, "The Power of Green," *New York Times*, April 15, 2007.

16. Zack Exley, author interview, December 2019.

17. Zoë Schlanger, "Alexandria Ocasio-Cortez's Climate Plan Is the Only One That Matches Scientific Consensus on the Environment," *Quartz*, June 27, 2018, https://qz.com/1316082/alexandria-ocasio-cortezs-green-new-deal-could-make-the-us-a-climate-change-leader/; Alexander C. Kaufman, "Alexandria Ocasio-Cortez Will Be the Leading Democrat on Climate Change," *Huffington Post*, June 27, 2018, https://www.huffpost.com/entry/ocasio-cortez-climate-change_n_5b3307a5e4b0b5e692f25e18.

18. David Freedlander, "One Year in Washington," *New York*, January 6, 2020, https://nymag.com/intelligencer/2020/01/aoc-first-year-in-washington.html.

EPILOGUE

1. "Transcript: Alexandria Ocasio-Cortez's DNC Remarks," CNN Politics, August 18, 2020, https://www.cnn.com/2020/08/18/politics/aoc-speech-transcript/index.html.

2. Mike Lillis, "Ocasio-Cortez Accosted by GOP Lawmaker over Remarks: 'That Kind of Confrontation Hasn't Ever Happened to Me,'" *The Hill*, July 21, 2020, https://thehill.com/homenews/house/508259-ocaasio-cortez-accosted-by-gop-lawmaker-over-remarks-that-kind-of.

3. Yahoo News, "AOC Says Yoho Made Excuses for Their Confrontation That She 'Could Not Let Go,'" July 23, 2020, https://news.yahoo.com/aoc-says-yoho-made-excuses-154306828.html.

4. Ina Fried, "AOC, Ilhan Omar Draw 400,000 to Twitch Stream to Get Out the Vote," *Axios*, October 21, 2020, https://www.axios.com/aoc-ilhan-omar-draw-400000-to-twitch-game-to-get-out-the-vote-2ff44af0-b60a-4906-8cda-648ae65e1242.html.

5. Associated Press, "Study: Fox News Is Obsessed with Alexandria Ocasio-Cortez," April 14, 2019, https://www.usatoday.com/story/life/tv/2019/04/14/study-fox-news-obsessed-alexandria-ocasio-cortez/3466493002.

6. *The Hill*, Twitter, November 10, 2020, https://twitter.com/thehill/status/1326313942864388096.

7. Alexandria Ocasio-Cortez, Twitter, November 10, 2020, https://twitter.com/AOC/status/1326265103960911872.